002.

Items should be returned on or before the date shown below. Items not already requested by other borrowers may be renewed in person, in writing or by telephone. To renew, please quote the number on the barcode label. To renew online a PIN is required. This can be requested at your local library.
Renew online @ **www.dublincitypubliclibraries.ie**
Fines charged for overdue items will include postage incurred in recovery.
Damage to or loss of items will be charged to the borrower.

Comhairle Cathrach
Bhaile Átha Cliath
Dublin City Council

Leaeharlanna Poiblí Chathair Bhaile Átha Cliath

Due Date	Due Date	Due Date
Brainse Rátheanaigh Raheny Branch Tel: 8315521		

IN SEARCH OF LOST BOOKS

In Search of Lost Books
Giorgio van Straten

TRANSLATED FROM THE
ITALIAN BY SIMON CARNELL
AND ERICA SEGRE

PUSHKIN PRESS

Pushkin Press
71–75 Shelton Street
London, WC2H 9JQ

In Search of Lost Books was first published as
Storie di libri perduti in Italy 2016

First published by Pushkin Press in 2017

1 3 5 7 9 8 6 4 2

ISBN: 978-1-78227-372-1

Typeset in Baskerville by
M Rules, London

Printed and bound by
T J International, Padstow, Cornwall

www.pushkinpress.com

Contents

INTRODUCTION:
THE RISK OF AN IMPOSSIBILITY   1

FLORENCE, 2010:
THE BOOK THAT I ACTUALLY READ
(BUT DID NOT PHOTOCOPY)   11

LONDON, 1824:
'SCANDALOUS' MEMOIRS   23

PARIS, 1922:
MEMORY IS THE BEST CRITIC   39

POLAND, 1942:
THE MESSIAH HAS ARRIVED IN SAMBOR   53

MOSCOW, 1852:
A 'DIVINE COMEDY' OF THE STEPPES   67

BRITISH COLUMBIA, 1944:
IT ISN'T EASY LIVING IN A CABIN   81

CATALONIA, 1940:
A HEAVY BLACK SUITCASE   95

LONDON, 1963:
I GUESS YOU COULD SAY I'VE A CALL   109

WORKS CITED   123

INDEX OF NAMES   127

IN SEARCH OF LOST BOOKS

Introduction:

The Risk of an Impossibility

T HIS IS MY JOURNEY in search of the traces of eight lost books as legendary as lode-bearing mines during the Gold Rush: everyone seeking them is convinced that they exist, and that they will be the one to find them, though in reality no one has certain proof of their existence, or reliable maps. In this case too, the clues are fragile, the hope of finding these pages scarce. And yet the journey is still worth undertaking.

Lost books are those that once existed but are no longer here.

They are not those forgotten books that, as happens to the majority of the works of mankind, gradually fade from the memories of those who have read them, slip from the histories of literature and then vanish, together with the existence of their authors. Books such as these can always be unearthed in some obscure corner of a library, or be re-printed by a curious publisher. Perhaps no one knows anything about them any longer. But they are still there.

Nor are they those books that were not even born: conceived, expected and dreamt of, but prevented for one reason or another from ever being written. In such cases we are also confronted by a lack, by a void that cannot be filled. But it's one created by notional works which never actually materialized.

For me, lost books are those an author did in fact write, even if they might not have been brought to completion: books that someone has seen, or even happened to read, but which were subsequently destroyed, or vanished leaving scarcely a trace.

The factors leading to their disappearance are extremely diverse. These texts may have fallen under the guillotine of the author's dissatisfaction, in pursuit of a kind of perfection that was impossible to achieve. No doubt it could be argued that if the author was so dissatisfied then perhaps we would have been so too – and that if certain contemporary writers were to experience such dissatisfaction with their own work, well, then we might all benefit from it. But then we find ourselves reading those books that someone has courageously rescued from the destructive will of an author – works by Kafka, for instance, in the most well-known case of this kind – and immediately realize how fortunate we have been that the writer's intentions were not respected.

In other cases the void was created by circumstantial and historical factors – above all during that conflict which spread everywhere without distinguishing between the battlefield and the home front, between combatants and civilians. Attempts to safeguard unpublished manuscripts during the Second World War, as we shall see, did not always turn out well.

In other instances it was censorship that intervened, including self-censorship, because the books involved seemed both scandalous and dangerous – and not only in a metaphorical sense, since in certain European countries in the nineteenth and even the twentieth centuries, homosexuality was a crime severely punishable by law.

It has also happened that some act of carelessness or forgetfulness caused a fire, or led to a theft (one that hardly profited the unwitting thieves: what, after all, was all that used paper good for?), resulting in the loss of years' worth of work and obliging an author to start all over again, if only they had the will and could muster the energy required to do so.

And then there are the wishes of the heirs and executors. In particular, those of an author's widow or widower determined to protect themselves or their children, or to safeguard the reputation of their husband or wife from incomplete as well as unpublished works, or to shield those persons still living who were recognizably portrayed in them.

In the eight cases that I will give an account of, there are examples of each of these factors leading to the disappearance of books. But the conclusion reached is always the same: the work searched for seems lost for ever, even though there is always a chance that someone, somewhere, at some time in the future...

Every time I have chanced across the story of a lost book I have experienced something like the feeling that gripped me as a child when reading certain novels which spoke of secret gardens, of mysterious cable-cars, of abandoned castles. I have recognized the opportunity for a quest, felt the fascination of that which escapes us – and the hope of becoming the hero who will be able to solve the mystery.

In those novels for children, the solution would invariably emerge towards the end of the book, obviously suggested by the author himself – though it seemed to me at the time to have resulted from my own concentrated attention, from my own imagination.

Of these eight lost books I have not managed to find a single one, or at least not in the conventional sense of the word 'find'. Only in the case related in the first chapter have I been in the position of actually being able to read one of these works *before* it was lost. Though even then I was not able to prevent its subsequent destruction.

Perhaps it is precisely because of this particular failure that I have decided to follow the clues towards other lost books, and to tell their stories, as if they were adventures. I first did this in a series of radio broadcasts, assisted by a few friends who were as passionate as I was about the authors and books chosen.

Together we explored the paths leading to their disappearance, consoled at least by the pages that had survived and that we could continue to read.

Later I decided to go back and retrace these same routes alone, as we do sometimes with places in which we have been happy, in the hope of recapturing the same feeling again – as well as to see if some clue that we had mistakenly overlooked might offer new insight into what had really occurred there. I have no doubt continued to stumble in the dark. Yet as frequently happens when travelling alone, I have indeed noticed things I had failed to see when walking in the company of others.

Each lost book has its own unique story. Yet there are also certain details that establish peculiar connections between them – between, for example, the cases of the Italian writer Romano Bilenchi and Sylvia Plath (an unfinished novel and a spouse who makes a fateful decision in the author's name); between Walter Benjamin and Bruno Schulz (born in the same year, both Jewish, both disappearing along with their last books during the Second World War), or between Nikolai Gogol and Malcolm Lowry (both wanting in their own way to write a *Divine Comedy*, both failing in the attempt). But what recurs most, with disturbing regularity, is fire. The fact that most of the lost works of which we are speaking were burnt reminds us

7

of their essential fragility. For we are dealing here with a period – the two centuries before our own – during which it was only paper that permitted the preservation of words written by men and women. And as we know only too well, paper burns easily.

We might think that today it is rather more difficult to *lose* a book, and that the numerous virtual supports we rely on to preserve them precludes the risk of anything being definitively destroyed. Yet it seems to me that this very immateriality may in certain cases prove to be as precarious as old-fashioned paper, and that those vessels freighted with words, which we launch onto the waters, in the hope that someone will notice them and receive them safely into their own harbour, can disappear into infinite space like spacecraft at the edge of the universe, receding from us at increasing velocity.

But these losses, anyway – are we sure that they are merely and exclusively just losses?

A little while ago I stumbled across an old notebook of mine in which I had written out certain passages I'd been struck by. There was one from Proust's *Remembrance of Things Past*:

One can feel an attraction towards a particular person. But to release that fount of sorrow, that sense of the irreparable, those agonies which prepare the way for love, there must be – and this is, perhaps, more than a person, the actual object which our passion seeks so anxiously to embrace – the risk of an impossibility.

What if the passion by which I am seized, by which we are all seized when encountering these lost books, had the same origin as this amorous one described by Proust? What if it were this very risk of an impossibility which justified that combination of impulse and melancholy, of curiosity and fascination, which develops with the thought of something that existed once but that we can no longer hold in our hands? Could it be the void itself which fascinates us, since it is possible to fill it with the notion that what is missing might be something crucial, perfect, incomparable?

These books also serve as challenges to our imagination, spurs to other writings, to the development of passions nourished by their very intangibility. It is no accident that many of these lost pages have ended up by prompting the writing of new books, of further ones.

But this is not all. There's something more besides.

In a novel from the end of the last century, *Fugitive Pieces* by the Canadian Anne Michaels, there is this:

There's no absence, if there remains the memory of absence. [...] If one no longer has land but has the memory of land, then one can make a map.

So this book is my own personal map, drawn from the memory of absent books which, with one exception, I have not been able to read. And since mapping was involved, when I was deciding in what order to relate these stories – whether to proceed chronologically, or alphabetically, or through internal links that would connect for the reader one case history with another – I decided in the end to choose geography: to chart a journey around the world in eight volumes rather than in eighty days. I started with the book that I failed personally to rescue, in my own home town of Florence, since its author also lived there – and went from there to London, the city to which like Phileas Fogg I also returned, after a circular journey passing through France, Poland, Russia, Canada and Spain.

By the end of the voyage I had realized that lost books possess something that others do not: they bequeath to those who have not read them the possibility of imagining them, of telling stories about them, of re-inventing them.

And if on the one hand they continue to elude us, to move further off the more we try to seize hold of them, on the other they come back to life in us – and ultimately, as in Proustian time, we can lay claim to having found them.

Florence, 2010:

The Book that I Actually Read
(but did not photocopy)

T HIS IS THE STORY OF A LOST BOOK about which I can give a direct testimony, since I am one of the four or five people who read it before it was destroyed.

No one will ever be able to do so again, and even the handful of those fortunate enough to have done so preserve only a memory of it that is destined, like all memories, to gradually fade and vanish with the passage of time.

But the story needs to be told from the beginning.

It is more than twenty-five years since the death of Romano Bilenchi. Though not widely recognized as such today, he was one of the great Italian writers of the twentieth century. I knew Romano and was very fond of him. We first met at the beginning of the 1980s when I was editing a collection of memoirs of the Italian Resistance for the Gramsci Institute in Tuscany. For this volume he had given me an unpublished account of his own experience as a partisan, and I continued subsequently to seek him out. I had also persuaded him to read my first immature attempts at fiction, and it was due to his encouragement that my first short story was published in a magazine called *Linea d'ombra*.

I only mention this personal connection to account for the fact that when his widow Maria Ferrara had regained the strength to begin putting her husband's papers in order, several months after his death in 1989, she called me to come and look at what she had discovered at the bottom of a drawer.

It was the manuscript of an unfinished novel. Its title was *The Avenue*. More than just unfinished, it had been left in an intermediate state between a first and second draft, and in the passage between them it had undergone significant, even contradictory changes. Maria was keen for me to read the work, and to discover what I thought of it.

I know that two other friends also read it at more or less the same time, and that a photocopy was given to the Manuscript Centre at the University of Pavia. Or rather to Maria Corti, who had collected there such a trove of works and letters by twentieth-century writers.

Reading it proved to be one of the most moving experiences of my life. Not least because I was discovering new writing by an author I loved, and one who had produced relatively little in his lifetime. These were the words of a friend and mentor whom I greatly missed. But there were other less personal reasons that served to make that reading so unforgettable.

Romano Bilenchi had published almost nothing between the appearance in 1941 of one of his masterpieces, *The Drought*, and the publication of *The Stalingrad Button* in 1972. Between these works there was a thirty-year hiatus, a period during which it seemed that he had been prevented from further creative writing not just by his professional activity as a journalist (until 1956 he was the editor of *Il Nuovo Corriere*, and was subsequently in charge of the cultural pages of the *Nazione* in Florence), but perhaps also by the contradiction between his own concept of literature – so deeply tied as it was to the process of memory, the psychological dynamics of interpersonal relationships, and especially to the period of transition between childhood and adulthood – and the hardline neorealist aesthetic propounded by the Communist Party to which he belonged until 1956.

He had returned his Party membership card immediately after the closure of the daily newspaper he was editing, a closure that was officially justified on economic grounds, but which was due in reality to the independent line it had always taken, and which became unambiguous during the summer of 1956 when the troops of the Warsaw Pact engaged in a bloody repression of protests by Polish workers. In an editorial, Bilenchi had come out in support of those protests and against the Soviet intervention, and it was this that had cost the *Nuovo Corriere* its existence.

In any case, whether due to his journalistic commitments or the clash between his own literary aesthetic and the prevailing tendencies of the official Left, it seemed certain that for thirty years he had not produced anything new, even though he had continued to write by repeatedly returning to earlier works such as *Anna and Bruno* and *The Conservatory of Santa Teresa*, almost obsessively recasting entire sections of them. Nothing of his had surfaced publicly, except for the odd short piece of prose published here and there, in magazines and in pamphlets for friends.

It was as if his desire to write fiction and his political commitment could not converge and be reconciled, and he had harboured a vision of literature so exacting and absolute that he was unable even to consider writing anything that was not entirely convincing in his own eyes.

To further justify this silence he had also alluded to drafts of works lost during the war, and in particular to an almost completed novel, the disappearance of which had blocked him for years. That novel was called *The Innocence of Teresa*, and though I obviously couldn't recognize the similarities at the time, there were many elements in his descriptions of this other lost work in common with *The Avenue*.

Roberto Bilenchi was a terse writer of marvellously lean prose, never given to a single excessive adjective. But as a teller of tales he was really loquacious, and the stories he told would often change over time, becoming embellished, transformed into literature. Consequently, it was difficult to take at face value everything he said, or many of the things he wrote in his highly imaginative letters. But when

16

he talked about that lost novel, perhaps he was also thinking about the manuscript actually lying, unknown to us,
at the bottom of a drawer in a cupboard in that very house
where he was speaking, and where his friends and disciples
were listening to him.

So here is the principal reason that made the existence
of that novel so important: it had been written in the years
1956–57 (the dates were recorded on its last page), and was
therefore situated at the heart of the thirty-year silence, a
period everyone had assumed to have been sterile ground
as far as the writing of new works was concerned.

Furthermore, it was a love story of the kind he had
never told in any of his previous works, or in any subsequent ones: the transposition of an actual clandestine
affair, of his relationship with Maria which began when
she was an editorial secretary at the *Nuovo Corriere* and his
first wife was still alive. And it was maybe because of this
that instead of coming to light it had remained shut away
in that drawer.

There was also a third point of interest. As mentioned,
Bilenchi's work had always been and would continue to be
based – in *The Stalingrad Button* and *Friends* – on the process
of memory: on narrative in which a long interval of years
had been interposed between the moment of writing and
the period referred to. In this case, on the contrary, the
narrative was almost akin to live reportage, and could be
directly compared to something that had just happened

or was still happening, even if the affair between the two lovers (called, perhaps, Sergio and Teresa, though I can't be sure) was probably also being conflated in part with the memory of the novel that was lost during the war.

It was a remarkable novel. Just holding it in my hands, recognizing on its pages – yellowed and slightly desiccated by the passage of years – the familiar handwriting of Romano, was a deeply emotional experience for me. I thought about making a photocopy in order to preserve those pages for myself. But my loyalty to Maria prevailed: she had made me promise to return it without duplication so that she would remain in unique possession of the work. It's the only time in my life that I have regretted acting honestly.

'If Romano did not finish it, and didn't publish it, then his intentions should be respected, and his reservations maintained': these were Maria's words when I met with her to return the manuscript. And she had a valid enough point. 'But it's equally true to say', I argued, 'that Romano did not discard the manuscript, did not destroy it, but chose to keep it instead. This seems to me just as significant. Perhaps he meant to take it up again when any potential cause of embarrassment had disappeared, when the people depicted in it were no longer around.'

With emotions similar to my own, the manuscript was read by two other friends of Romano's: the writer Claudio Piersanti and the literary scholar and editorial director Benedetta Centovalli. They had also been sworn to secrecy, and were faithful to the request not to photocopy it. Benedetta even read it in Maria's home. I can't say for sure if anyone else got to hold it in their hands, though perhaps the poet Mario Luzi did.

All three of us were in agreement that it was not possible to publish it separately in its incomplete form as novel, but we were also convinced that it was crucial to any critical reading of Bilenchi's work. It should be included in an edition of his Complete Works, or at the very least be made available for scholars to consult in manuscript.

When we expressed our opinion to Maria she raised no objection, but neither did she indicate any kind of agreement. She kept her own counsel and bided her time. Eventually all mention of it was dropped. For years, almost twenty in fact, I forgot all about it. Or rather I consigned the memory of that novel to a corner of my mind, waiting for the right moment to speak of it again, including publicly.

Then, in the spring of 2010, Maria died. A conference on her husband's work had been scheduled to take place just a few days later at the Gabinetto Vieusseux in Florence. We wondered how to react, before eventually deciding to go ahead with the event, dedicating it to her.

In my own lecture I dwelt on the great strength of the rapport between Maria and Romano, describing it as a love story that had been lived rather than written, though I also let it be known that there was an as yet unpublished work by him in which, albeit with literary license, he had attempted to give an account of that love.

After I had delivered my paper I was taken aside by Benedetta Centovalli, who told me quietly that the novel was gone.

'What do you mean *gone*?' I replied. 'Maria kept it in her home. I'm sure that somewhere or other there...'

But no: before her death she had decided to burn their letters to each other, together with the manuscript of the novel.

'But what about the photocopy that was given to the library in Pavia?' I asked, hoping that at least this facsimile had been saved.

'She'd asked Maria Corti to return it to her, years ago. Even that copy is gone.'

It's difficult to enter into the minds of others, or to judge right from wrong in such situations. No doubt personal letters and diaries are such intimate documents that a husband, wife or child has the right to do with them as they see fit. But a novel that the author has deliberately preserved, if only by shutting it away in a drawer?

Maria rightly considered her husband to be one of the great Italian writers of the last century, and had always respected his judgment, even when she didn't agree with it. Despite her admiration for his first book, *The Life of Pisto*, for example, she had complied with his own repudiation of it, refusing to allow it to be re-issued as a single volume after his death. So how can I suppose that she would have done anything detrimental to his work, and to literature?

I don't think that her decision to destroy *The Avenue* was exclusively due to the fact that it dealt with actual events, with existing persons. In the end, only the people involved can recognize in a literary text the traces of actual life: the only person who could have been hurt by *The Avenue* was her husband's first wife, and she had died decades ago.

If the author had not destroyed it himself, or asked someone else to do so, why make it disappear forever, preventing anyone from reading it in the future?

It's worth repeating: it's difficult to enter into the minds of others.

With affection and admiration, Maria had stayed close to Roberto Bilenchi over many years, including through the long years of the illness that eventually killed him, and after his death she had never assumed the insufferable role of the widow who takes it upon herself to determine the truth about her husband, controlling that which may or may not be said about him. She had always remained reticent and detached, though never indifferent.

Yet she ended up by committing an act which prevented the possibility of reading a novel, albeit an unfinished one, that he had decided to leave to posterity.

Why had she chosen to do this?

I returned to the subject in conversation with Benedetta Centovalli, not in order to apportion blame but to understand the reason behind this drastic act and knowing that, as in the case of a suicide, the explanations we find are almost always banal, partial, and inadequate. What was it that Maria feared, if the manuscript had been allowed to survive? What possible harm to Bilenchi could it have caused?

Benedetta told me about the phone call during which Maria had informed her that she had destroyed the letters and the manuscript just a few months before her death. Benedetta had said to her that she could hardly believe it. But Maria insisted: she had destroyed them. And to this day Benedetta remains convinced that she did indeed act on her decision to do so.

In that decision, arrived at after years of reflection, Benedetta sees an extreme gesture of love, probably prompted by the unfinished state of the novel – a crucial factor for a writer such as Bilenchi, always in search of precision, of *le mot juste*, of the eminently well written. For him, an unfinished book was probably not a book at all. I tell her that I understand, yet continue to think that Maria did not have the right to destroy it.

We could go on discussing the issue at length, but about one point we are in definite agreement: in all of us, as followers of Bilenchi, there remains a bitterness about a novel that no longer exists, and which is fading irrevocably from our memories of it.

London, 1824:

'Scandalous' Memoirs

THIS IS A STORY ABOUT CENSORSHIP. Not the kind of censorship engineered by the state against an opponent of a regime, or used by religious authorities to regulate the moral health of a community. But rather a preventive intervention made by friends of the victim in order to avoid, apparently, the outbreak of a scandal and ruinous damage to his reputation. Yet it is censorship, nonetheless, that we are dealing with – of the more furtive and insidious kind, originating as it does in a capitulation to convention and public opinion.

We are in London, in May 1824: George Gordon, Lord Byron, died a month ago in Missolonghi, where he had gone in the hope of adding to his enormous fame as a poet that of a freedom fighter in the cause of Greek independence.

We are in Albemarle Street, in the office of his publisher, the first John Murray. (I add 'the first' since he was followed by an unbroken sequence of other John Murrays, down to the seventh, who after finally giving

25

different names to his sons sold the publishing house and its archive in 2000). In the office with Murray are John Cam Hobhouse, a friend of Byron's since his student days at Cambridge and now the executor of his estate; his half-sister, closest relative and former lover Augusta Leigh, along with another close friend, the poet Thomas Moore. Amongst the few others present is the lawyer representing the interests of Byron's estranged wife, the mother of his only legitimate daughter.

Hobhouse and Augusta Leigh are convinced that it is necessary to burn the manuscript of the *Memoirs* Byron had written a few years previously and given to his publisher for an advance of two thousand pounds. The text had reached Murray via Moore – and this, as we shall see, was hardly by chance.

The publisher has some qualms, and hesitates – then gives in. He agrees to the destruction of the manuscript on condition that the advance should be returned to him. Augusta Leigh hands over the money necessary to keep him quiet. Only Thomas Moore resists, convinced that even if the *Memoirs* should not be published immediately it would be wrong to destroy them, to lose those pages in which Byron had used his tremendous prose to reveal so much about himself, his life and his passions. In the days leading up to this meeting the discussions between Moore and Hobhouse had been so heated that they almost ended in blows.

There can hardly be any doubt that Moore was right to defend the work. Not least because it could be argued, with hindsight, that whilst some of his poetry has become difficult to appreciate (especially the longer poems, with the notable exception of *Don Juan*), his direct and spontaneous prose, graced by an extraordinary rhythm, can be readily enjoyed even by contemporary readers. And so to have saved the *Memoirs* (their original title) would have been to bequeath that considerable pleasure to future generations.

But apart from poor Moore, sadly, everyone was in agreement that such scandalous and dangerous pages as these were should be made to vanish forever.

I do not suppose that Byron needs much introduction as the personification of one type of Romantic figure: precocious, tenebrous (satirically represented by Thomas Love Peacock as 'Mr Cypress', after the tree most typical of cemeteries), bursting with talent and vital energy; recklessly profligate with himself and a great serial seducer; both sentimental and heroic; determined to leave his mark not just on literature but on the history of humanity itself. A man whose charm had for years proved irresistible – to both men and women alike – even if at the time of his death, at just thirty-six years old, he was overweight, almost completely bald and had bad teeth, with little remaining of the outstandingly handsome figure that has been handed down to us in the portraits.

So what did these *Memoirs* contain, so very scandalous that it was not enough merely to conceal them, that made it necessary to destroy them altogether, erase them as if they had never been written?

Perhaps it was an account of his short-lived and ill-fated marriage to Anne Isabella Milbanke, the marriage that had given him a daughter but which had foundered after only eleven months, ending in acrimony and recrimination. Perhaps it was his incestuous love for his half-sister Augusta, which according to the gossip that circulated in London (and was apparently stoked by Byron himself) had been the real reason for the failure of his marriage.

Either subject would have sufficed, especially the first, since it is not difficult to imagine with what magisterial malice Byron might have depicted a wife who had been so little loved, and who since their separation had resorted to every means possible to take her revenge.

Yet it seems that the real source of potential scandal lay elsewhere. And that the unpardonable shame that would have emerged from those pages, in a more or less explicit way, was that of Byron's homosexuality: the monstrous vice, the crime that could not be confessed, however widely it was practised in England at the time. Despite the fact that homophobia continues to manifest itself in so many forms and contexts, it is difficult to conceive of the views that were held in nineteenth-century Britain regarding consensual sexual relations between two adults of the same gender.

Those found guilty of committing such acts were liable to be pilloried, and subsequently hanged, though only if the first punishment – exposure in the stocks to 'public opprobrium', but also to any object which that public saw fit to fling in the face of the condemned – had not already had a conclusive effect. And although in 1861 it ceased to be a capital offence, it was still punished severely for many years to come, as notoriously demonstrated on the threshold of the twentieth century by the case of Oscar Wilde.

The scandal caused by the exposure of homosexual relationships led to suicides, flights abroad, and cases which at best would culminate in complete and irrevocable ostracism from public life, and from all social relations, with the guilty exiled to the countryside to find consolation in some clandestine rural relationship. The more well-known the transgressor, the greater the scandal that was generated.

Byron was at the time of his death one of the most famous, well-loved and most highly paid of English poets. Ever since the publication of *Childe Harold's Pilgrimage*, his literary and worldly success had been phenomenal. But in parallel to the growth of his fame as a poet, the rumours about his alleged homosexual relations had multiplied and grown louder. Precisely because of this, following advice from his half-sister Augusta, he had entered into a marriage of convenience: one which not only failed to silence the rumours but which, on account of if its brief nature, actually ended up fuelling them – thanks largely, it seems, to a neglected wife and a frustrated lover.

And so Byron had eventually been obliged to resort to something very like a flight into exile: when he left England in 1816, he already knew that in all likelihood he would never return.

After a long pilgrimage through continental Europe he stopped in Venice, where he found tolerance and openness – an atmosphere possible only where there was no substantial English community to contend with. (The presence of this community, by contrast, had curtailed his stays in Florence and in Rome.) In Venice he began a period of intense poetic productivity and started working on the *Memoirs* – they were for the most part written during this stay, between 1817 and 1818, and subsequently expanded between 1820 and 1821 – and all of this industry from a man with a renowned facility with the pen makes one suspect that, when completed, they must have amounted to a work of considerable substance and length.

In all of Byron's works it is possible to detect traces of his personal experience: journeys, thoughts, acquaintances and encounters – but with the *Memoirs* it was a case of putting his experience down more directly onto the page, of revealing himself as he had never done before. Because of the very nature of the form, he had probably ended up revealing his homosexuality.

I say 'probably' because here, as in the rest of this book, I am referring to something that has disappeared. But the eyewitness accounts of it, however reticent, are nevertheless all in basic agreement on this point.

So perhaps we should be asking instead how Byron might have chosen to disclose this side of himself, and this aspect of his life. He was fully aware of the fact that it was difficult to broach the subject in a work intended for publication in England. He may have been thinking if not of a posthumous edition then of one intended for some indefinite future date. But he cannot have failed to consider the prospect of publication: why else would he have sent the *Memoirs* to his publisher, and have secured from him an advance of two thousand pounds?

Because if it's true that despite earning vast sums Byron was constantly in need of money and therefore willing to hand over any of his writings in exchange for a fee, I doubt whether John Murray, who I do not take for any kind of philanthropist, would have been willing to countenance such a large advance for a work that was not deemed publishable even by its author.

How can we reconcile the idea of a homosexual Byron with the image that we have inherited of him as a kind of irresistible *homme fatale*, an irrepressible serial seducer of women?

There's no doubt that he was a relentless seducer – of women, with whom he had innumerable affairs – but also of men, especially very young men, as had been the case amongst his Cambridge companions of old. From the days of his studies and travels abroad, the first of these with Hobhouse, Byron's relationship to sex was always characterized by excess and abundance. His true orientation, or most prevalent tastes, might therefore have been hidden amongst his kaleidoscopic adventures with the opposite sex.

Hobhouse himself had been one of Byron's lovers in his early youth, as had the Trinity chorister John Edleston. Despite the fact that Edleston died young, having met the poet only once after their time at Cambridge together, he would always remain Byron's favourite

So it is understandable that in mid May of 1824, when the news of Byron's death reached London, Hobhouse was more than a little concerned about the *Memoirs* that were in the hands of his publisher. Concerned, that is, not just for his friend's reputation but also about his own. Perhaps primarily about his own, since by now he had entered politics and become a Member of Parliament.

After all, it had been Hobhouse who had convinced Byron, on returning from their first trip abroad, to destroy a diary in case someone might cast an eye over it at the English border. Precisely at that time in fact, John Edleston, one of those who figured prominently in Byron's diary, was arrested during a police raid in Hyde Park. Yet Byron would later deeply regret his decision to destroy the diary – surely a factor in his choice of Moore rather than Hobhouse to deliver the *Memoirs* to Murray. Given such a precedent, he could hardly have relied on Hobhouse to do so.

Aware of the sensitive material they contained, as he relates in his *Detached Thoughts*, the *Memoirs* had in any case already undergone a 'cleansing', so to speak, by Byron himself. But perhaps this authorial intervention did not go nearly far enough, and almost certainly would not have done from Hobhouse's point of view.

Self-censorship, erasures, pre-emptive redactions: the spectre of the stocks and of the gallows hung constantly above their heads.

In England, the social climate regarding homosexuality was such that even in the middle of the twentieth century, John Murray (I can't tell which one this time) allowed the Byron scholar Leslie Marchand to access his firm's archive only on condition that he would make no reference to this aspect of the poet's life. Only in his biography of Byron published in the 1970s was he able to make some vague reference to his sexual preferences – and only then because finally, in 1967 (not until then!), homosexual acts between consenting adults had been decriminalized in the United Kingdom.

We have already touched on the fact that Byron was careful to conceal behind a licit – or at any rate heterosexual – relationship, the other kind that dare not speak its name. Even in *Manfred*, the work that perhaps deals most directly with the impossibility of living freely with one's desires, Byron dramatizes that impossibility by resorting to the metaphor of incestuous love. The kind, that is, that he had for his half-sister Augusta, and would use to conceal the real reasons behind the break-up of his marriage.

The writer and poet Franco Buffoni has devoted a novel to retelling the story of the author of *Don Juan*. Published a few years ago, *Byron's Servant* is narrated from the point of view of a manservant who gives an account of his master's life, filling in the gaps left by the *Memoirs*. Although as he says at one point:

> [...] I have read my master's *Memoirs* from start to finish, every word of them: my only regret is that I did not secretly copy them, thus saving them from disaster. Only my memory of them remains. I am able, undoubtedly, to relate the facts – but alas not to reconstruct the style of my Lord. And in literature, as is well known, style is everything.

Buffoni helps me to understand, amongst other things, the various types of relationship Byron was capable of weaving. He tells me that today we have the vocabulary to do so, distinguishing between sexual orientation and sexual behaviour. His behaviour was bisexual and extremely promiscuous, full of Don Giovanni-esque adventures (no wonder he wrote *Don Juan*, the mock-epic poem devoted to the figure of the all-conquering seducer) with aristocratic women and wenches – from 'La Fornarina' in Venice (his housekeeper as well as his mistress) to countesses such as Teresa Gamba Guiccioli (despite being secretly infatuated with her brother) – with young men and prostitutes. And his behaviour was the same wherever he went. Whether it was in the Ottoman Empire, which he would fight against in Greece, or in Albania; whether in Italy or Malta: there was always an opportunity for his compulsive collecting of liaisons of every type. But his orientation, his true love, was always for very young men: from one of the first, John Edleston, to the last, Lukas Chalandritsanos, whom he met during his Greek adventure and who, when faced with the imminent death of the poet, fled with money intended to pay soldiers engaged in the rebellion.

Now that we can read Byron's letters, at least in part, it seems clear that his deepest emotions were always elicited by male figures. But it is also true, for reasons already alluded to, that as long as he was in England he was not only subject to censorship but to self-censorship, as seen in the changes made to the diaries. His circumspection when writing the letters extended to the use of coded allusions in Latin and Greek, and to elisions designed to confound all but their intended recipient.

This is why, when he felt safe in Italy and his amorous exertions were at their peak, he was able to allow himself the freedom to write his *Memoirs*, almost as if he were bringing a phase of his life to a close, perhaps the one in which he had been happiest. Though it could hardly be said that he possessed there, like the longed-for woman in his poem *She Walks in Beauty*:

> A mind at peace with all below
> A heart whose love is innocent.

The afflictions of the heart that he would subsequently experience in the wake of the Venetian period would not be the same; his physical deterioration would undermine his capacity to seduce, and his vital energies would be directed towards the destined-to-fail struggle for Greek independence.

Let's return to the office of his publisher, on that day in May 1824. A May that was unseasonably cold and wet.

Thomas Moore still puts up a fight, seeking to prevent the work written by his colleague and friend from being fed into the fire: what amounts to condemnation to a second death, it seems to him. But by now he is alone in defending it.

I would like to have been there by his side. To have invited the people gathered there to consider a quite different proposal: by all means put the text away somewhere under lock and key, on condition that it should not see daylight for a hundred or even two hundred years. But don't destroy it. The right to protect individuals is sacrosanct, but so is the need to preserve works of literature: the imperatives can converge and be compatible, if you only want them to. Byron had made sure that these *Memoirs* would reach his publisher and I can hardly believe, as some have argued, that he did so primarily in order to get back at his ex-wife. He wanted them to be survive and to be published: his will should be respected!

But I am not there, and the others only have Moore left to convince.

In order to achieve this they offer to assign to him the first, authorized biography of his friend. He will even be allowed to paraphrase parts of the *Memoirs*, and to go so far as to cite extracts (though when he was to do so, certain terms deemed too *risqué* would be hidden by asterisks), just as long as he excluded even the vaguest reference to same-sex relationships. In the end Moore gives in and allows himself to be bought, though in his case not for money, as it had been for Byron's publisher. The biography will come out in 1830.

And so the bundle of papers ends up in John Murray's fireplace. It is hard to imagine which one of those present would have had the courage to feed them into the flames. Not Murray himself, who had returned the manuscript. It is unlikely to have been the pusillanimous Hobhouse. We can dismiss the idea that the task was given to a woman

37

to perform. Thomas Moore would not have accepted such a role: we can imagine him leaving the room, unable to witness the destruction. It is possible that the task fell in the end to a subordinate office worker, an ordinary and unwitting employee of the publishing house. Or alternatively to the legal representative of the author's widow, someone who was sure to have secretly rejoiced in the act.

What is beyond doubt, unfortunately, is that in May 1824 Byron's *Memoirs* were lost for ever.

Paris, 1922:

Memory Is the Best Critic

S HOULD WE SIMPLY TRUST WRITERS when they claim that something of theirs has disappeared; that complete or nearly finished novels or short stories have been lost in outlandish circumstances, making it necessary for them to be started over again from scratch?

There are so many stories of this type, so similar in their fundamentals, that we are inclined to question them. Like Doubting Thomases of literature, we find ourselves requiring some tangible proof, or at the very least eyewitness accounts dating back to the period in which the supposed event took place.

And what should we think if the blame for the loss is attributed to a spouse? To a first wife, for instance, who was to be followed by another three wives and who therefore no longer seems worth defending? Especially since, in the circumstances of this case, she seems to be the perfect scapegoat?

Yet what if the writer in question, if not exactly known to be a *blagueur*, is nevertheless renowned for projecting an

41

image of himself as being beyond the pale, lost between wars and love affairs and travels? Would it not be advisable to take his account with a pinch of salt?

But instead of asking so many questions beforehand, it is probably better just to tell the story, and see what comes of it.

We are in Paris, towards the end of 1922, and we are dealing with a story about a suitcase. It will not be the only time that what is about to occur will do so in the course of this book. This particular suitcase is where it is meant to be just before departure: on an overhead rack in a train standing in the Gare du Lyon. But the woman who has put it there is suddenly overcome by such an irresistible thirst that she leaves her compartment and gets down to quickly grab a bottle of *Evian*. And when she gets back on board, the case has vanished.

That suitcase contains all of the first attempts at fiction, including an entire novel, by one of the great writers of the twentieth century, Ernest Hemingway, and the woman from whom it was stolen was his first wife, Hadley Richardson.

It is Hemingway himself who tells the tale writing that 'My Old Man' – the story that Edward O'Brien included in the annual *Best American Short Stories*, bending the rules to do so since it had not been previously published – was one of only two texts to have survived after everything he'd written had been stolen along with Hadley's suitcase at the station. She had decided to bring his manuscripts with her, so that he could continue working on them while they were holidaying in the mountains. In that suitcase, according to Hemingway, she had placed everything: the manuscripts, the typewritten versions, and all the carbon copies as well. 'My Old Man' survived only because he had sent it to an editor who'd returned it together with a letter of rejection. This copy of the story was recovered from the pile of unopened mail Hadley had left in Paris. The only other text to have survived this theft was 'Up in Michigan', a story Hemingway had given to Gertrude Stein to read and, receiving from her such a negative response – she deemed it to be *inaccrochable*, as if it were a painting that should not be hung – filed away separately at the bottom of a drawer.

After the incident on the train, he travelled down from Switzerland to Italy, and submitted 'My Old Man' to O'Brien in Rapallo, where he was living at the time. But let's turn to Hemingway's own account of the scene:

> It was a bad time and I did not think I could write any more then, and I showed the story to him as a curiosity, as you might show, stupidly, the binnacle of a ship you had lost in some incredible way, or as you might pick up your booted foot if it had been amputated after a crash and make some joke about it.

Then, when he read the story, I saw he was hurt far more than I was. I had never seen anyone hurt by a thing other than death or unbearable suffering except Hadley when she told me about the things being gone. She cried and cried and could not tell me. I told her that no matter what the dreadful thing was that had happened nothing could be that bad, and whatever it was, it was alright and not to worry. We would work it out. Then, finally, she told me. I was sure she could not have brought the carbons too and I hired someone to cover for me on my newspaper job, I was making good money then at journalism, and took the train for Paris. It was true alright and I remember what I did in the night after I let myself into the flat and found it was true. That was over now and Chink had taught me never to discuss casualties so I told O'Brien not to feel so badly. It was probably good for me to lose early work and I told him all that stuff you feed the troops. I was going to start writing stories again I said and, as I said it, only trying to lie so that he would not feel so badly, I knew that it was true.

This is how Hemingway tells it many years after the event, in *A Moveable Feast*, an incomplete memoir written towards the end of his life and published posthumously. And it almost seems in this version of events as if Hadley and O'Brien were the ones who had been most affected by the loss. Much more so than the writer himself. But that reference to the conviction that he would never be able to write again? It shows the extent to which it had been, in truth, a really traumatic event for Hemingway.

Hadley Richardson, a young woman from Saint Louis, was twenty-eight when she met a young Hemingway barely into his twenties. With her square face and reddish hair, she was not conventionally beautiful. Yet when he evokes her in these pages written towards the end of his life, she represents for Hemingway everything he had lost during the course of the years and had not been able to recover with any of his subsequent wives: something much more valuable than the stolen papers. The story he had decided to relate was not just about a suitcase full of manuscripts which had been stolen from a railway station. It was about the apprenticeship of a writer: pages and pages that had disappeared in the space of a few minutes, with no hope of ever finding them again. Even with your whole life still ahead of you, this is a hard blow to take, since until you are sure of your vocation any such incident might turn out to be enough to make you give up.

I have already mentioned the degree of caution necessary when dealing with memoirs written years after the event – but *A Moveable Feast* actually derived from a series of notebooks that, together with a number of other things, Hemingway had put into two trunks and left at the Paris Ritz at the end of the thirties. They were returned to him in November 1956, when the trunks were discovered in storage by the hotel manager – and the fact that the published memoir was underwritten by these contemporary diaries allows us to give it more credence. It is surely also worth pointing out here that Hemingway did have a marked tendency to lose or to forget things...

During the period when the suitcase was lost, Hemingway was living in Lausanne and working as the European correspondent for the *Toronto Star*. The texts Hadley had wanted to bring to him were part of an attempt to find out if he was capable of writing fiction in parallel with his work as a journalist, and to see if such writing might form part of his future career.

Of all the stories I cover in this book, Hemingway's is certainly the one I am inclined to take most lightly, since the lost pages do not represent the irreparable destruction of something that could never be rewritten – but simply a beginning that came to a bad end. And it is always possible that a lost beginning might be followed by another and better one.

Nevertheless, for Hemingway it represented a real tragedy, ushering in the end of his youth and the beginning of a period of uncertainty as to what might follow. The illusory hope that Hadley might only have taken some of the material, and that in their home in Paris carbon copies might still be found reveals the panic he felt at the time, and the seriousness of the situation. Yet Hadley, in her haste before leaving, had indeed bundled together all of his papers, without making any kind of selection. Discriminating between them was something that could be done by her husband when she caught up with him.

It appears that Hemingway advertised a reward for the return of his suitcase. It was obvious that whilst for him the contents of that case represented the fruits of more than three years' labour, for a thief they would be just so much useless paper. But nothing came of it. Evidently the thief did not read notices in newspapers. The suitcase was never recovered.

These first attempts at fiction were apparently marked by flaws, in particular by an excess of lyricism, according to certain allusions Hemingway made to them in retrospect, and if we are to set any store by Gertrude Stein's reaction to 'Up in Michigan'. If we consider how every sheet or scrap of paper of his has been deemed publishable since his death, it is possible to conclude that in some cases it can be fortuitous if certain unpublished apprentice writings are lost. But the fact remains that at the time they disappeared, when he was uncertain whether he would ever write anything other than journalism, the theft of the suitcase had the potential to be completely destabilizing.

That the loss for Hemingway was indeed a real and even traumatic one is evidenced by a letter he wrote shortly afterwards, in January 1923, to Ezra Pound:

I suppose you heard about the loss of my Juvenilia?...
You, naturally, would say "Good" etc. But don't say
it to me. I ain't yet reached that mood. 3 years on the
damn stuff.

And in fact Pound in his reply, ignoring his friend's plea
not to put a positive spin on the loss, characterized it as
an act of God and advised him to use his recollection of
the work – to recover from it what was worth recovering,
since 'memory is the best critic'. But is memory really the
best critic? Is it really possible to remember in its entirety
something you have written but no longer have to hand?
It is one thing to recall a sensation, an idea, a phrase –
quite another to reproduce page after page of what was
actually written, perhaps arduously enough in the first
place. Correcting, rereading, finally managing to hit the
mark: who is ever in a position to completely recover such
a process simply by remembering it?

Besides, if there was an entire novel amongst the lost
work, as there was according to Hemingway in *A Moveable
Feast* – 'the first novel that I had written' – how could
resorting to memory possibly begin to suffice?

Yet the fact is that this novel had not been going well. It
was drenched with 'facile adolescent lyricism', and therefore it was 'a good thing that it had been lost'. At least this
is how Hemingway would remember it a decade later,
eventually agreeing with Pound. It was quite a different

novel that he would go on to write – *Fiesta*, published in 1926 – and it would take him a good while to complete.

If you are strong enough and in robust health – albeit frequently hungry for want of funds to purchase even a good meal, as Hemingway was in these years – then anything is possible, everything can be recovered, even if it means starting over again and reinventing from scratch.

It is likely therefore that the upset was indeed more significant for Hadley, since she could not have known for certain that her husband would start writing again, even if she was the one who in these years had believed unwaveringly in his talent, supporting him throughout the course of his apprenticeship. It was not Hadley who had the inner strength to resolve that everything could not only begin again but could actually do so for the better.

Perhaps Hemingway reflected on this when he again came into possession of those old notebooks discovered by the manager of the Ritz in Paris, and on rereading them rediscovered the flavour of those years, of the youth that had gone forever, as well as the wife who had been abandoned decades ago and who now seemed to be the weak link, the guilty one – but also the primary victim of these events.

It turns out that *A Moveable Feast* might well have had a different title, according to my friend Lorenzo Pavolini, the writer from whom I have gleaned some valuable information. Before choosing one of them, Hemingway would always devise several potential titles for his books. In this case, one of those potential titles was *How Different It Was When You Were Here.* How different everything was indeed. And yet he seems to be saying that it was precisely at this time, in this far-off and forgotten era, that he actually succeeded in becoming a writer.

For reasons located somewhere between literary criticism and gossip, it would be intriguing to be able to peruse those lost papers, to revisit the origins of a master storyteller, however riddled they might be with errors and even horrors. It would be like wandering around the laboratory of someone who has not yet attained the formula you know they will soon succeed in finding. Because even if it is true that certain writers achieve 'overnight' success and even fame, it is equally true that they have become the particular writers they are only through a long and arduous process.

In April 1961, three weeks before a failed suicide attempt and not long before the one that would kill him, Hemingway wrote:

> In writing there are many secrets. Nothing is ever lost no matter how it seems at the time and what is left out will always show and make the strength of what is left in.
>
> Some say that in writing you can never possess anything until you have given it away or, if you are in

50

a hurry, you may have to throw it away. In much later times than these stories of Paris you may not have it ever until you state it in fiction and then you will have to throw it away or it will be stolen again.

Is the use of the word 'stolen' a mere coincidence? Or did Hemingway when writing it think again about that train compartment, about his first wife's sudden thirst, about a suitcase that a thief would dump the moment he discovered its contents were worthless? And about the dash back to Paris, only to find that even the carbon copies could not be salvaged?

He must have thought again about his first wife, and about the fruits of that apprenticeship, which none of us will ever be able to read.

Poland, 1942:

The Messiah Has Arrived in Sambor

A MAN KILLS ANOTHER MAN'S SLAVE in order to spite him.

We are not standing in the shadow of the pyramids, or in ancient Rome, or in a plantation in Louisiana before the War of Seccession. We are in Europe: the year is 1942, the place a small Polish village with the almost illegible name of Drohobycz, which I give thus because at the time it was part of Poland, though it is now part of Ukraine and would be written differently. The two men are Nazi officers: one is called Felix Landau, the other Karl Gunther. They have argued, and in order to assert himself and save face with his opponent, Gunther has murdered his slave, or rather his protégé – a diminutive Polish Jew whom Landau had taken under his wing because he liked his drawings, and had charged him with creating some murals in the bedrooms of his children.

This small Jewish man who was so good at drawing was in fact not only one of the greatest Polish writers of the twentieth century but one of the greatest in Europe. His name was Bruno Schulz.

He had been born precisely fifty years earlier, in 1892, in that very place from which he had rarely moved except for three years spent in Vienna, and he had published two volumes of short stories – *Cinnamon Shops* (1934) and *Sanatorium Under the Sign of the Hourglass* (1937) – books in which he had described the life of the small town in which he lived, the myriad characters who made up its petty, captivating, banal and magical world, depicted in a vein that was fabular and oneiric but also anxiety-inducing and angst-ridden.

Like a cross, in short, between Chagall and Kafka.

'A gnome, a tiny man with a disproportionately large head, too timid to have the courage to exist, rejected by life, one who moved furtively at its margins': this is how he was described by Witold Gombrowicz, his colleague and friend, if we can call this the description of a friend. And yet this unprepossessing and marginal person was a truly extraordinary writer.

Since the mid-nineteen-thirties, Schulz had been at work on a novel called *The Messiah* – a novel he considered to be his *magnum opus* and which disappeared together with its author in 1942, in the heart of Poland, after a stupid altercation between two German officers.

In what I consider to be his masterpiece, *See Under: Love*, the novelist David Grossman writes:

People hear I'm interested in Bruno and send me all kinds of material. You'd be surprised how much has been written about him. Mostly in Polish. And I've come across a number of theories concerning his lost novel, *The Messiah*: that it's about how Bruno lures the Messiah into the Drohobycz Ghetto with his spellbinding prose, or that it's about the Holocaust and Bruno's last years under the Nazi Occupation. But you and I know better, don't we? Life is what interested Bruno. Simple, everyday life; for him the Holocaust was a laboratory gone mad, accelerating and intensifying human processes a hundredfold...

Part of this novel is dedicated to Schulz, albeit a Schulz who in the narrative has been transformed into a fish – or more precisely into a salmon, swimming back upstream against the current of seas and rivers.

In addition to the story of his remarkable life, this lost work by Bruno Schulz has inspired many writers. Cynthia Ozick has written a novel about *The Messiah* and its mysterious reappearance in Stockholm – we shall see how fiction sometimes anticipates reality – and there is a work by the Italian writer Ugo Riccarelli entitled *A Man Called Schulz, Perhaps*. It often happens that lost books have the potential to generate new ones, prompting other writers to fill the void that has been created in their wake. But the task of the writer, as Mario Vargas Llosa once remarked, consists of 'lying with good reason'. And not only when transforming Bruno Schulz into a fish.

But are we really sure, as Grossman suggests, that *The Messiah* disappeared without anyone having ever set eyes on it?

Before seeking an answer to this question, let's try to establish whether the book ever actually existed in the first place.

Bruno Schulz lets it be known that he is working on it in a series of letters written between 1934 and 1939. From these letters we also gather that for him it was *the* Novel, with a real capital N; something that had come after a period of great difficulty, partly caused by the breakup of his engagement to Josefina Szelinska, after she had failed to convince him to leave his native town to go and live with her in Warsaw. Amongst other things, this relationship had led him to question his Jewish faith, to the extent that he had even considered converting to Catholicism, without knowing that his fiancée was herself a convert. It was probably the breakup of this relationship that caused a rapprochement with the faith of his forefathers, with that Jewish culture which gives central importance to the Messiah who has yet to come.

Another factor confirms that the novel not only existed but was nearing completion: the important Polish critic and intellectual Artur Sandauer, a friend of Schulz's, has said that in 1936, during a vacation, the writer had read the beginning of the book to him. It went something like this:

> You know, my mother told me one morning that the Messiah has come, that he is already in the village of Sambor.

Sambor was a village very close to Drohobycz.

So we know that the novel existed. And there is more, if further proof were needed. It is possible in fact to actually read two of its chapters, 'The Book' and 'The Genial Age', which perhaps because they were complete and convincing in themselves, or simply extracted to bolster the collection, were included as free-standing stories in *Sanatorium Under the Sign of the Hourglass*. These two stories allow us to glimpse the visionary dimension that the novel must have had, in common with the characteristics of his other fiction.

And then there are the illustrations, since this novel was intended to be illustrated by Schulz himself, an exceptional visual artist as well as a writer. Though the word 'illustrated' here is inadequate: drawings and text were intended to work together as integral parts of the narrative, in a kind of graphic novel *avant la lettre*, so to speak. A number of these images from *The Messiah* have survived and come down to us, bearing further testimony to his work on the novel.

The fact that writing and drawing were for Schulz part of the same creative impulse was made clear in an interview given in 1935 to his friend and fellow writer Stanisław Ignacy Witkiewicz:

> To the question as to whether my drawings manifest the same themes as my prose I would answer in the affirmative: they deal with different aspects of the same reality, [...] the technique of drawing imposes more narrow limits than prose, which is why I think that I express myself more fully in writing.

And it is those very drawings that allow us to understand Schulz's world: an archaic, impoverished and static Jewish world very far removed from that of the Jews of Western Europe, and about to be swept away by the Nazi invasion, as Schulz himself seemed already to foresee in 1938 in the last of his stories to be published in his lifetime, 'The Comet':

> One day, on returning from school, my brother brought the improbable but perfectly true news that an end of the world was near. We asked him to repeat what he said, thinking that we must have misunderstood. But we had not.

The Messiah existed, there can be no doubt about it. It was finished, or nearly finished when the news arrived – 'improbable but true' – that war had broken out and that Poland would be erased from the political geography of Europe, divided into two by the Molotov-Ribbentrop pact, with one part going to the Soviet Union and the other to Nazi Germany. Drohobycz found itself on the Russian side of this dividing line.

During the period of the Soviet occupation, having seemingly already stopped writing in 1939, Schulz put many things away into safekeeping – entrusting them in particular to his colleague and friend Kazimierz Truchanowski. Some think that he also gave him the manuscript of *The Messiah*, though Schulz himself always denied this.

Then, with the German invasion of the Soviet Union in August 1941, Drohobycz came under Nazi control. From that moment on, the theories proliferate as to what Schulz did with his novel. Some maintain that the typescript was buried in a garden, others that it was hidden inside a wall; still others insist that it was concealed beneath the tiles of a floor. And so on, because many Jewish writers resorted to hiding their texts in this way in order to save them. At least one such hastily concealed manuscript was rediscovered decades later, and if I may be permitted a digression it is worth relating its story here.

In 1978, in the course of renovating a property in Radom in Poland, two workmen found inside a wall they were demolishing a bottle containing strips of paper that had been written on in Yiddish. Their author was one Simha Guterman, and he had not survived the persecution. He had written a novel dealing directly with the lives of Polish Jews under Nazism, and had gradually concealed segments of it in various places, indicating their whereabouts to his son Yakov so that he might remember and recover them. His son survived the war and emigrated to Israel, but when he returned to Poland he had not been able to locate the nooks and crannies chosen by his father: a question of memory, no doubt, but also due to the fact that the country had been largely destroyed and rebuilt. Nevertheless, a single section re-emerged, thirty years later, thanks to workmen who decided not to discard along with the rubbish the paper-filled bottle they had found. And today we can read at least a part of that novel.

The Messiah, however, has not turned up during some work of reconstruction in Drohobycz, and it is certain that amongst the many materials belonging to Schulz that have been patiently collected over the years by the Polish poet and scholar Jerzy Ficowski (the letters, drawings, notes that have contributed to the postwar rediscovery of the writer), his only novel is not to be found.

*

Many of the things I have mentioned thus far came to me courtesy of Francesco Cataluccio, a passionate and insightful scholar of Polish culture, as his book *I'm Going to See If Things Are Better Over There* demonstrates. He has shared with me everything he has discovered about Bruno Schulz over the course of many years. But the most incredible thing he had to tell me only emerged in the latest of my conversations with him.

As already mentioned, one of the books devoted to Schulz and his lost novel is Cynthia Ozick's *The Messiah of Stockholm*. In this novel, published in 1987, the American author imagines that a man who believes himself to be Schulz's son comes into contact in an antiquarian bookshop in Stockholm with a strange woman who claims that she has the manuscript of *The Messiah* in her possession. This manuscript will eventually be lost again – or rather burned by the person who considers it to be a forgery – but the protagonist will continue to ask himself whether it had really been *that* book.

Well, a few years after the fall of the Soviet empire, at the beginning of the 1990s, the historian Bronisław Geremek (who was Polish Minister of Foreign Affairs at the time) told Francesco Cataluccio about having been approached by a Swedish diplomat with news of an astonishing proposal. This diplomat had been contacted in Kiev (Drohobycz, remember, is now part of Ukraine) by a former agent of the KGB, or at any rate someone who claimed to be one and maintained that in the archives of the secret police there was a typescript of *The Messiah* by Bruno Schulz. And that if the Swedish government was interested, or could act as an intermediary with the government of Poland, he would be willing to sell it. Geremek managed to obtain a page of this typescript so that it could be examined by experts, including Jerzy Ficowski, in order to determine its authenticity. Their verdict was that it might actually be part of *The Messiah*. At which point the Swedish diplomat was given the funds necessary to acquire the text, and travelled with the required sum to the Ukraine.

Perhaps he did in fact obtain the typescript, perhaps not. We cannot know for certain, since on his journey back the car in which he was travelling crashed and caught fire, killing both the diplomat and his driver.

How the crash happened, and whether it was indeed an accident or something more sinister, it's impossible to tell. Nor do we know whether the typescript was inside the car and therefore burned, as it was in Ozick's novel – or if the diplomat was returning empty-handed, leaving open the possibility that, somewhere, it is still extant. Always assuming, of course, that the whole thing was not simply a scam, concocted in those confused and turbulent times in order to earn a sizeable sum of American dollars.

Since then many have contacted Ficowski or the

executor of Schulz's literary estate (the son of his brother, now living in Switzerland), claiming to have the manuscript in their possession. But not a single one of these communications has ever come to anything.

Moscow, 1852:

A *Divine Comedy* of the Steppes

I N ALL OF THE CASES that I have dealt with thus far, the disappearance of the lost books in question could hardly be attributed to those who actually wrote them, or to some culpable carelessness or involuntary complicity on the part of the author, as will turn out to be the case with Malcolm Lowry.

In the story that I am relating here, however, it was the author's very perfectionism, his desire to give to the world something superior to everything and everyone that had gone before him – an incomparable masterpiece – that doomed the work to inevitable failure. It was this very desire to produce a flawless work of art, one that could combine his thinking about both literature and morality, which ended up by precipitating a human as well as a creative tragedy.

I am referring to Nikolai Gogol, one of the greats of nineteenth-century Russian literature and the author of such unforgettable stories as 'The Overcoat' and 'The Nose', and above all, the novel *Dead Souls*. It is this novel that is the victim of the story I am about to tell.

Dead Souls can be found in any bookshop, yet what we are able to read under that title is in reality only the first part of what should have been a much longer work, designed to be even more impressive in scope. Five chapters of a second part have survived and are frequently included in an appendix to the book we have, but they represent only a first draft that was abandoned by its author out of dissatisfaction with the work. According to Gogol's conception of the novel, it should in fact have been tripartite – like a kind of *Divine Comedy* of the steppes – with an Inferno, a Purgatory and a Paradise.

In the first part, the one published in the author's lifetime, the protagonist Chichikov presents himself in a small provincial Russian town with the aim of acquiring 'dead souls' – that is to say serfs who have passed on to a better life but are still present in the census of the State, and for whom, consequently, their owners are still obliged to pay tax. What on earth can he be doing with them? Why is he buying them up? Everybody wants to know. Yet everyone is nevertheless quite willing to profit from selling them, in order to save on their taxes. And Chichikov profits substantially too, by mortgaging these nonexistent souls to raise capital to invest and to spend.

Gogol based the story on a notorious case related to him by Pushkin, who was apparently somewhat annoyed by his friend's subsequent creative appropriation of it.

The first volume of *Dead Souls* came out in 1842,

originally published for reasons of censorship under the title *The Adventures of Chichikov, or Dead Souls*, since by definition souls were immortal and when combined with this adjective were better off being relegated to a subtitle. It was a resounding success. It was also an impossible book to categorize: brilliant, ironic, grotesque, realistic; all of these things at once. It was praised superlatively and attacked; vilified by reactionary critics and admired in the most progressive literary circles. Receiving the eulogies with what must have been an already healthy sense of his talent and its importance, Gogol began to think of himself as the greatest of them all: a kind of literary messiah sent to guide the people of Russia onto the right path. And it was this, perhaps, that caused him to lose his own way.

Perfectionism and self-sabotage: Gogol had always been prone to both. When he was just eighteen years old he had published a long poem in a small provincial magazine, and when confronted with negative critical reactions to it had bought up every copy of the magazine he could lay his hands on and burnt the lot.

In the case of *Dead Souls*, however, not only were there no negative reactions from any of the critics whose opinions he respected – on the contrary, too many expectations had been raised about what was to come next. He decided to take stock, and to bide his time.

He began to travel in Europe, above all in Germany

and in Italy, writing and discarding what he had written as he went; writing and rewriting as if everything that came from his pen could never be completely satisfactory. The five surviving chapters are the result of a confusion of different drafts which somehow escaped another emancipatory bonfire of papers lit by Gogol around 1845, and which it is impossible for me and difficult even for the most informed scholars to reconstruct. Though some maintain there never was such a fire, and that the chapters actually come from a ledger that had simply been forgotten by their author.

In any case, even if the Russian writer was never satisfied with what he had committed to paper, there can be no doubt that he was in fact writing. We have from 1849, for instance, a testimony that at the house of one Alexandra Smirnova certain chapters of a new draft of the second part of the novel had been read. Or rather, of the poem, as Gogol was now calling it with Russian peculiarity, just as Pushkin called his poem *Eugene Onegin* a novel.

In short, in the midst of the enormous confusion generated by multiple drafts and by the continuous travelling that must have contributed to his fluctuating physical and mental health, the only certain thing is that at some point the second volume of *Dead Souls* disappeared.

We are in Moscow, on the evening between the eleventh and twelfth of February, 1852, ten days before the death of the author. (According, that is, to the Orthodox calendar, which at the time diverged by ten days from our own, so that the outbreak of the October Revolution actually occurred in our November.) Gogol is a guest at the house of a friend: one Count Tolstoy, but not the writer of the same name. The only account of what now takes place is given by his manservant – an actual manservant this time, rather than the kind invented by Franco Buffoni in order to testify to the lost work of Byron – a young man called Semyon who was barely thirteen years old at the time.

The account given by Semyon, if we decide to believe it, is excruciating. Gogol asks for a folder to be brought to him, and takes from it a bundle of around five hundred pages tied together with a ribbon. In front of his manservant he opens the door of the stove (or was it a fireplace?) and throws the bundle of papers into the fire. 'Master!', Semyon cries, 'What are you doing? Stop!' Gogol responds curtly: 'It's none of your business. Pray instead!' But the pages tightly bound by the ribbon do not burn. So Gogol retrieves them from the stove or fireplace, unties the ribbon and begins to feed them in a few at a time, lighting them with the flame from a candle. Now they burn readily. When they have all been consumed by the fire, Gogol stretches himself out on the bed and begins to weep.

Serena Vitale, an extraordinary scholar of all things Russian to whom I am indebted for much of the information I have about this case, including about what took place in that room in Moscow in 1852, has told me that 'This is the first of many bonfires that punctuate the history of Russian literature in the nineteenth and twentieth centuries, due to authorial dissatisfaction or for reasons of censorship: Dostoyevsky (with the first draft of *The Idiot*), Pasternak, Bulgakov, Anna Akhmatova.'

And then she cites something by Marina Tsvetaeva which gives a markedly symbolic reading of this particular literary conflagration:

The poet? A sleeper. One who has woken up. The man with the aquiline nose and the waxen features who burns a manuscript in the fireplace of a house in Seremetev. The second part of *Dead Souls*. [...] That half-hour of Gogol's at the fireplace has done more in favour of good, and against evil, than all Tolstoy's many years of preaching.

In favour of good and against evil (that is to say, art), because that fire had a great deal to do with a mystical and religious crisis, almost an overwhelming neurosis that had afflicted Gogol, and that together with his literary dissatisfaction had been the reason for a self-loathing accompanied by ascetic rituals and fasting under the guidance of a severe archpriest called Matvej Konstantinowski, one of the many tutelary figures of the powerful and of artists that punctuate the life of Russia, culminating in the rise of Rasputin under the last Tsar.

And so the picture clarifies: at the root of his decision to destroy the second part of *Dead Souls* was not only his enormous literary ambition, the idea that this was to be an immortal masterpiece of Russian literature, but also the desire to edify, to construct a grand cathedral dedicated to nothing less than the moral reconstruction of the Russian people.

And this takes us to the heart of Gogol's problem: for if with his grotesque realism he had been able to depict an inferno of mediocrity, how could he use the same literary means in order to construct both a purgatory and a paradise of the steppes?

It appears, moreover, that Konstantinowski had repeatedly urged him to renounce his art, to abandon that corrupt and imperfect literary world, that sublime malady that was antithetical to the fulsome health of faith. And perhaps, in the end, Gogol had acquiesced.

In moving towards such a decision, the circle of Slavophiles surrounding Gogol also played a significant role: Slavophiles with their commitment to the triad of Orthodoxy, Tsarism and Autocracy. A circle of reactionary admirers who guided him onto a terrain – politics – that turned out to be far from his proper one, and led him to become the author of embarrassing political articles.

The destruction of the missing parts of *Dead Souls* may

well have had its origins in his crisis of faith, and an infat-
uation with anti-Western European ideology (even as he
found himself to be so much better off in Rome...).

But there are other theories regarding its loss. That
he had burnt it, for instance, according to one Russian
source (and this is what happens when you accumulate
too many drafts!) by simply confusing a subsequent version with an earlier one he wanted to get rid of. A scarcely
credible hypothesis, however much his failing health might
have affected his actions. After the fire he will live on for
another ten days, but only in a kind of prolonged agony,
without ever wanting to touch food again, tormented by
the useless cures of the doctors (plunged into cold baths,
festooned with leeches, etc.), in a state of utter despair.

Others maintain that no such bonfire occurred because
there was in truth no manuscript to burn in it, and that
the whole episode had simply been invented by his servant.
Others still, in the Russian tradition that sees conspiracies
everywhere, contend that the manuscript was removed by
his enemies. Which ones? And why? Perhaps it was taken
by those reactionary Slavophiles who did not want his
conversion to be sullied by a text that was at odds with
and even contradicted it? Or perhaps by the perfidious
democrats, who would have destroyed this hymn to rural
and Orthodox Russia, this paean to the enemy of the
secularized West?

If this were the case (and it is not the first time I have

encountered similar theories in relation to my lost books), then perhaps the manuscript may still exist somewhere: hidden away but liable, sooner or later, to come to light again.

'I don't believe it,' Serena Vitale tells me. 'But if the day should come when it does,' she adds, laughing, 'even if it's after I'm gone, I'll come back from the other side to read it.'

One question remains. Was it completed, or was it still unfinished?

Maybe where Gogol is concerned – with his maniacal perfectionism, his continuous corrections and doubts about what he had achieved, his constant rewriting and revisions – nothing was ever really concluded. It is hardly surprising that testimonies regarding his public readings refer only to the first few chapters, with which he was reasonably satisfied. And yet I am convinced by the theory that a second volume was substantially there at the time of his death; that it was almost finished.

And so perhaps, beyond the religious crises and political intrigue, the real motive for destroying the book, and the one most in keeping with Gogol's innermost character, is that the author failed to find a way of bringing to redemption his engaging anti-hero, the scoundrel Chichikov; that he failed to find a way of giving verisimilitude to 'good' characters, of making them convincing. The more extraordinarily deft his touch in depicting irredeemable fraudsters, in exposing the mediocrity of the provincial landowners, the little monsters of great Russia, the weaker it became when dealing with the ways of the upright and the just. It was as if he was lost for words when faced with describing such rectitude – even if he aspired to it himself – just as Chichikov becomes speechless in the novel when faced by the wise and capable squire Kostanzoglo.

Is it not therefore, in the end, the same problem Dostoyevsky will experience, with his own difficulty in matching his great sinners with equally compelling descriptions of good men? The same problem which, with its earnest desire to be edifying, socialist realism will not be able to solve?

Perhaps Tolstoy was right after all when he wrote in a diary entry of 28 August 1857: 'I have read the second part of *Dead Souls*; it's half-baked.' He was clearly referring to the first five chapters, the only text we have to assess how Gogol was attempting to resolve the problem, and I still feel humbly disinclined to concur with such a thorough-going dismissal as Tolstoy's.

This was the draft that Gogol himself deemed to have been superseded, even though it turned out to be the only one to survive his compulsive perfectionism.

If I may be permitted an attempt to summarize the situation in which Gogol found himself: it was his religious ideals that pulled the work towards a Dantesque conception of redemption after the fall; it was loyalty to his art that pushed him to destroy everything that did not achieve the high standards he set for himself.

So we could reply to Tsvetaeva: in the fire that consumed *Dead Souls* what prevailed, perhaps, was art. Even if, knowing Gogol, it is probable that from those lost pages, despite everything, the traces of a tremendous talent would nevertheless have emerged.

Tsvetaeva also writes:

Perhaps the second part of *Dead Souls* would not have convinced us. But it would surely have given us joy.

British Columbia, 1944:

It Isn't Easy Living in a Cabin

THE PARADIGM OF THE *poète maudit* is difficult to dislodge. Many continue to believe that a disordered life full of excess and adventure forms the basis on which the talented can construct who knows what marvels. We only need to think of musicians – jazz musicians in particular, but also those rock stars of the sixties and seventies – so many of whom were convinced that dropping out was inherently more interesting than leading a bourgeois life, and that drink and drugs would have a positive effect on their creativity, only to discover that the exact opposite was the case: after an initial period of euphoria and apparent expansion of their powers of invention, there followed depression, stupefaction, physical decline. How many stories of this kind could be told: from Bix Beiderbecke to Charlie Parker, and from Janis Joplin to Jimi Hendrix.

The same goes for writers, since often the tale of their tumultuous lives has ended up diminishing their literary talent. Or, because of those lives they have achieved a dubious fame.

Lived outside of the usual boundaries, these disordered and chaotic lives often enough had destructive consequences for the works of those who led them: not only because of the difficulty of establishing productive working routines, or of completing work once it had been started, but because of the relative ease with which it could be damaged or lost amidst such confusion. A tendency towards self-destructiveness hardly inspires a desire to conserve the things we have created.

Into this category of doomed or damned artists Malcolm Lowry might be conscripted, due to his now legendary consumption of alcohol, and the fact that by some it has even been intimately connected with his very style of writing. As far as I'm concerned, however, I remain convinced that Lowry himself never subscribed to the idea that dependence on alcohol enabled him to write better. On the contrary, all that drinking was the result of an existential malaise he had struggled with since adolescence (he had started to drink to excess at the age of fourteen), and the act of writing constituted a daily battle against that terrible and unquenchable dependence. That said, there was unquestionably in his difficult existence a destructive tendency directed both towards himself and towards his own writings.

We have only two books that were published in Lowry's lifetime: *Ultramarine*, and the novel unanimously considered to be his best work and an absolute masterpiece: *Under the Volcano.* Some other works have been published posthumously, put together from unfinished material and first drafts, which were always intended to be followed by others. But another novel, reputedly of over a thousand pages in length and called *In Ballast to the White Sea,* seems to have been definitively lost, though I will account for that 'seems' in my conclusion to what follows.

Lowry was born in 1909, the son of a rich cotton merchant. From the outset his life seems to have oscillated between trying to gratify his family – at fifteen he won a junior National Golf Championship, subsequently went to Cambridge University in accordance with his mother's wishes, and did not resist his father's determination to make him join the family firm – and a longing for independence and detachment which caused him to go to sea as an ordinary seaman on a merchant ship. It was in Oslo during one of his journeys that he met the poet Nordahl Grieg, a peculiar Norwegian Stalinist who became the inspiration for his first novel, *Ultramarine.* There are those who maintain that this book was plagiarized from the writings of Grieg, as Lowry himself partially admitted in a letter to the Scandinavian author:

> Much in *Ultramarine* is a paraphrase, a plagiarism, or a parody of what you have written.

Between one drinking bout and another Lowry had managed to lose even this first novel. Or rather someone had stolen it together with the suitcase that had been flung onto the back seat of his publisher's convertible, parked in front of a bar. As luck would have it, a friend who had typed up the final version of the novel, and clearly knew who he was dealing with, was able to supply a carbon copy he had retrieved from a bin in Lowry's home.

After having returned to England and concluded his studies at Cambridge, Lowry escaped again, this time to continental Europe; in Spain he met the writer Jan Gabrial and married her in Paris in 1934 before travelling with her to Mexico and the United States. These continuous displacements were the outward, visible signs of his incurable restlessness.

Though they loved each other deeply, Gabrial eventually decided to leave him, explaining later that life with Lowry was impossible unless you were a cross between a mother and a nurse – neither role she considered herself cut out for. Theirs proved to be a brief enough story, already over by 1937. And yet Lowry would never recover from the sense of bereavement he felt at losing her: as is clearly evident when reading *Under the Volcano*, she was the love of his life.

In 1938, having remained there alone after Jan had abandoned him for someone else, Lowry left Mexico (or to be more precise, was expelled) and went to Los Angeles, still tormented by the demons of writing and alcoholism. He lived there in a hotel which his father had begun to pay for directly after discovering that the money he sent to his son was being spent on drink. It was in Los Angeles that he met his second wife, Margerie Bonner, an aspiring writer who had been a silent film actress as a child and who would take care of him for the rest of his life, with the kind of single-minded devotedness that Gabrial had been understandably unwilling to give.

From Los Angeles they moved to Vancouver (where Margerie joined him with the typescript of *Under the Volcano* which Lowry, true to form, had left behind in California), and from there to Dollarton, a village in British Columbia where they lived from 1940 to 1954, in a kind of squatter's cabin without electricity or running water.

This was the cabin that was to burn down in 1944, destroying the only copy of *In Ballast to the White Sea* – the book Lowry had worked on for nine years. It had been an undertaking requiring such effort and dedication that he could not begin to think of starting it over again.

The grand idea that he had been working on was of composing a kind of drunken *Divine Comedy*, a trilogy of novels entitled *The Voyage that Never Ends*.

If *Under the Volcano* was his Inferno (and what could be more infernal, after all, than the smoking summit of Popocatepetl), then *In Ballast to the White Sea* was his Paradise, with water representing the element of purification and liberation, in contrast to the fires of *Volcano*. The Purgatory was meant to be a third novel, published posthumously in 1968 in an incomplete draft form entitled *Lunar Caustic*, and more recently under the title *Swinging the Maelstrom*.

Lowry's Paradise is a marine one, as the very title of *In Ballast* indicates. The term 'in ballast' refers to a ship travelling without cargo, carrying only the weights necessary to stabilize it, on its voyage *towards* the White Sea. The White Sea is a southern inlet of the glacial waters of the Barents Sea; the territories surrounding it are all Russian, and on its shore rises the city of Archangelsk. And this, together with information in letters and from other sources, alerts us to the fact that forming the basis of the novel is the same politico-existential mythology that Lowry had derived from his contact with Nordahl Grieg, and that fascinated him during the writing of *Ultramarine*.

According to some, Lowry's basic idea had been to combine the English socialism of the Cambridge intellectuals with the mythic Nordic vision of the Norwegian poet: two elements that were probably incompatible, especially in light of the appropriation of Aryan mythology by the Nazis that so terrified the writer, but which was sidestepped by him, so to speak, in a deft and masterful way. It made for an extraordinary bundle of elements, worthy enough of Lowry at his best.

On the website of Ottawa University Press (later on

we shall see why there in particular), it says that the novel would have featured a Cambridge student who wants to become a writer but who comes to realize that his book and in some way even his life had already been written by a Norwegian novelist: an ingenious reversal of what Lowry had inflicted on Grieg in *Ultramarine*!

On the other hand, if the novel was one thousand pages long it must have contained a good deal more than this, accompanied as always by the brilliant verbal acrobatics of Lowry's signature style.

The problem was that after nine years it was still not finished, perhaps due to the difficulty that a demonic writer such as Lowry must have had in writing his own Paradise: the same difficulty we have seen with Gogol, and one which might explain the length of time taken, the rewritings, the enormous accumulation of material. Then, in 1944, the shack in Dollarton burnt down.

A few years ago two friends of mine, both writers and enthusiastic admirers of Lowry, went to Dollarton together: Sandro Veronesi on a journalistic assignment, Edoardo Nessi at his own expense and out of sheer passion for the English writer. It was they who put me on to the story of *In Ballast to the White Sea*, urging me to include it in my journey in search of lost books.

Sandro gave me an account of that expedition to one of the ends of the earth, where nothing remained of Lowry's presence other than a memorial stone where the cabin once stood. We are in the vicinity of Vancouver, on the bay of Burrard. Lowry lived there, as I have mentioned, for almost fifteen years: writing, trying to drink less, swimming in the freezing sea. There were tall trees and beaches – and nothing else. It was the most westerly place in the world, and one of the furthest away from Nazism.

'Who knows what we had hoped to find,' Sandro says to me, 'but when we arrived we saw that there was really nothing: only shacks such as those on the banks of the Po for fishing with drop-nets, not places for living in. And yet he had spent so much time there, attended to by the saintly Margerie, in a place where even supplying himself with alcohol must have been rather more complicated than in London or New York.'

After the cabin burnt down there were further fires in two other shacks that had been built as replacements, which significantly damaged, if not destroyed them altogether. We know about these subsequent fires from Lowry's own confusing and imprecise accounts.

And quite a few other things do not add up. How, for instance, can he have been working for nine years on a manuscript that was destroyed in 1944? Had he actually started writing the Paradise section before the Inferno? And why did Margerie not think of keeping a copy of it, since she must have been fully aware of his previous experiences with manuscripts? It does prompt us to wonder whether the manuscript ever actually existed.

Instead of this text we have only a few surviving fragments which are preserved as relics by the University of British Columbia: small pieces of paper with burnt edges, like maps of pirate treasure.

The last line of the fragment which I have seen on a webpage reads:

now he had hours, hours more...

But precisely what Lowry lacked after the fire was the time, as well as the strength, to begin over again a novel of more than a thousand pages. And we can easily understand his reluctance to do so, given that his circumstances were also progressively deteriorating, and that the very success he had achieved with *Under the Volcano* turned out to be counterproductive, inciting him to start travelling again – to leave Dollarton, where he had managed to give so much of himself to writing and was settled. Even if the place in which he had settled happened to be in British Columbia and he had next to no money there, relying exclusively on a small allowance from his father whilst being cared for, encouraged, and supported by his wife.

Sandro Veronesi tells me that many years ago, when he was the editor of *Nuovi Argomenti*, he published an issue of the review devoted to Lowry. It included a number of letters and recollections, including one supplied by his doctor. With the detachment of a man of science, he described the characteristics of someone suffering from – we might almost say handicapped by – an illness. Lowry constructed his texts by dictating them: he could not write due to the trembling of his hands. Standing, he would rub his knuckles on the table in a compulsive gesture until they bled. Every act of composition (and I feel the musical term is apt) entailed for him both physical and mental torment.

And it was distressing for anyone to witness this state of illness and suffering, even for his doctor: the suffering of a man who was also a kind of genius. Unquestionably, a genius.

I had almost finished writing this book when, surfing the internet in my customary search for some ultimate lead regarding my lost volumes (I called them this as if they were the Lost Boys and I was their Peter Pan), I came across the most startling news: Ottawa University Press had announced the forthcoming autumn publication of *In Ballast to the White Sea*.

I started a further frantic online search: one of my lost books had been found! I soon discovered that its editor was already touring the world giving lectures about it. One of these was scheduled to take place in Norway, and was devoted to the novel's Nordic elements.

I asked myself whether I should exclude this chapter from my book. I was both pleased and disconcerted by the prospect.

In fact, however, this Canadian publication of *In Ballast to the White Sea* is a draft version rediscovered amongst the papers donated to a university in the United States by Jan Gabrial. It was the first draft of the novel which the couple had left with her mother before setting out for Mexico. Dating more or less, that is, from 1936.

Therefore it is not our book, Eduardo Nessi replies, when I send him the links necessary to examine the news.

It definitely is not. Also extant, for instance, is a draft of *Under the Volcano* that is quite different from the book published by Lowry in 1947. The text in question is one of the innumerable unfinished manuscripts left behind by the author, perhaps deliberately, perhaps not. And we immediately wonder how he could have lost all recollection of it, and never thought of going to look for it after the fire. But this is the first and only case in this journey of mine in which something once lost has resurfaced. It provides more significant proof than a few charred slips of paper that the book actually existed – and that it is possible, even likely, that the subsequent version of more than one thousand pages was indeed located in that Canadian shack.

It also makes me think that there is perhaps no one in the world, not even a man in the best of health, who would be capable of writing the same novel a third time.

Catalonia, 1940:

A Heavy Black Suitcase

THE LIFE OF WALTER BENJAMIN came to an end on the 24th of September 1940 in a small town called Portbou on the border between France and Spain. And it was Benjamin who decided to end it.

It is surely strange to think that one of the greatest intellectuals of the twentieth century and a man associated with two of the major capital cities of Europe should find himself constrained to make such a choice, or rather to endure his destiny, in a place so marginal and remote.

When I write that he was one of the greatest intellectuals of the twentieth century I am certainly not exaggerating, though I feel I should add another qualifying adjective to define him: European, because if there is a man who thought of himself as being so, in those years when Europe was only a geographical term, it was undoubtedly Benjamin; pushed to move from one nation to another not only by events and because he was a Jew and therefore subject to persecution, but also on account of his interests and restless curiosity.

Born in Charlottenberg in Germany in 1892, after the Nuremberg Laws Benjamin was forced to move to France. Its capital city became a kind of second homeland for him, and the site of his intellectual passions – to the extent that one of his major works, the unfinished *The Arcades Project*, would be entirely devoted to nineteenth-century Paris.

I think Benjamin is a wholly exceptional figure. It is difficult to find anyone else who was able to combine encyclopaedic erudition and a real gusto for accumulating material and ideas with the sophistication that more frequently goes with being an epigone (one tasked with concluding itineraries rather than opening up new ones) – and with his capacity to innovate, to read the world in a new light, to capture the first signs and elements of the momentous epochal changes that were to come. Those who revolutionize are not typically overly concerned with style – but rather with the need for rupture, destruction and re-invention unhampered by linguistic preoccupations.

Yet Benjamin was a consummately refined revolutionary.

He was the one who first understood, for instance, that the possibility of making multiple copies of a work of art through mechanical reproduction, so that it could be viewed without having to be physically present in the place where it is preserved and displayed, would consequently divest this work of its *aura* – a combination of distance, singularity and wonder that signalled the superiority of the artist in relation to the world.

What was this sophisticated and creative intellectual, this deep-rooted denizen of capital cities, doing there in that small town on the border between Spain and France? And what is it that gives him a place in my search: which book of his was lost? Because it will have been guessed by now that if I have followed him to this point, to where the slopes of the Pyrenees descend into Catalonia, it has been to discover what happened to the typescript he was carrying in a heavy black suitcase from which he never wanted to be separated.

Let's go back a few months. Since 1933, Benjamin had been living in Paris with his sister Dora. But in May 1940, after a period with no movement on the front between France and Germany, the German troops invaded neutral Belgium and Holland, proceeding rapidly and encountering little resistance as they did so, largely due to the surprise nature of attack from this direction. They would enter Paris on June 14, 1940. The day before – just the day before – Benjamin had decided to leave the city that he loved but that was rapidly turning into a trap for him.

Before leaving, he gave to Georges Bataille – a writer and intellectual as innovative and enquiring in his way as Benjamin himself – the photocopy of his great unfinished work on Paris, *The Arcades Project*. Or perhaps we should say *ur*-photocopy, since it was the outcome of the first attempts to reproduce documents photographically. The existence of this copy is of significance here, because even if the aforementioned black suitcase had contained the original of this work, the fact that a reproduction of it had been left with Bataille would hardly justify the anxious attachment Benjamin evidently felt towards this item of luggage.

When Benjamin left Paris he had a plan: to reach Marseille, and in possession of the permit allowing him to emigrate to the United States, which his friends Theodor Adorno and Max Horkheimer had managed to obtain for him, to go from Marseille to Portugal and embark from there for America.

Benjamin was not an old man – he was only forty-eight years old – even if the years weighed more heavily at the time than they do now. But he was tired and unwell (his friends called him 'Old Benj'); he suffered from asthma, had already had one heart attack and had always been unsuited to much physical activity, accustomed as he was to spending his time either with his books or in erudite conversation. For him, every move, every physical undertaking represented a kind of trauma, yet his vicissitudes had over the years necessitated some twenty-eight changes of address. And in addition he was bad at coping with the mundane aspects of life, the prosaic necessities of everyday living.

Hannah Arendt repeated with reference to Benjamin remarks made by Jacques Rivière about Proust:

> He died of the same inexperience that permitted him to write his works. He died of ignorance of the world,

because he did not know how to make a fire or open a window.

before adding to them a remark of her own:

With a precision suggesting a sleepwalker his clumsiness invariably guided him to the very centre of a misfortune.

Now this man seemingly inept in the everyday business of living found himself having to move in the midst of war, in a country on the verge of collapse, in hopeless confusion.

Miraculously, after long forced delays, in stages only completed with extreme difficulty, Benjamin nevertheless managed, at the end of August, to reach Marseille – a city that had become the crossroads for thousands of refugees and desperate people attempting to flee the fate pursuing them. In order to survive, to leave the city, it was necessary to have document after document: in the first place a residence permit for France, then a permit to leave the country, then another to travel through Spain and Portugal, and finally one allowing entrance to the United States. Benjamin felt overwhelmed.

In addition, to return to Arendt's phrase about misfortune, he had always been convinced that it had pursued him – like the 'little hunchback' of German folklore, a harbinger of bad luck, a jinx causing his victims to bungle and to fail. He had already experienced many instances of such misfortune: from his failure to get onto the first rung of the academic ladder with his work *The Origin of German Tragic Drama* (a work nobody had understood) to the fact that in order to escape the bombing of Paris he so feared, he had moved to the outlying districts of the city and unwittingly ended up in a small village that was one of the first to be destroyed. Benjamin had not realized this apparently insignificant place was at the centre of an important rail network, and therefore liable to be targeted.

In Marseille he managed to sort a few things out. He gave Arendt the typescript of his 'Theses on the Philosophy of History' so she could deliver it to his friends Horkheimer and Adorno (so this work could not have been in the black suitcase either) and collected his visa for the United States. But he lacked one crucial document: the exit visa from France, which he was unable to request from the authorities without marking himself out as a refugee from Germany, and thus being immediately referred to the Gestapo.

Only one option remained: to cross over into Spain via the Lister route, so named after the commander of the Spanish republican troops who had used it, albeit in the opposite direction, to lead part of his brigade to safety at the end of the Civil War.

This was suggested to Benjamin by his old friend, Hans Fittko, whom he had encountered by chance in Marseille.

Fittko's wife Lisa, then in Port Vendres near the border with Spain, was helping others who found themselves in the same situation to get across. So Benjamin set out, along with a photographer called Henny Gurland and her sixteen-year-old son Joseph. They formed a haphazard and totally unprepared group.

They arrived at Port Vendres on September 24. And on that same day, guided by Lisa Fittko, they covered the first section of the route in a trial run.

But when the time came to turn back, Benjamin decided not to go with the others. He would wait there until the next morning, when they would resume their onward journey together, since he was very tired and would in this way save himself the extra exertion required to go back and return. 'There' consisted of a small pine copse. Physically exhausted and disheartened, Benjamin remained there alone, and it is difficult to imagine how he must have spent that night: whether prey to his anxieties or calmed by the nocturnal silence beneath the star-studded Mediterranean sky, so distant from the chill of a German autumn.

The next morning he was joined soon after daybreak by his travelling companions. The path they took climbed ever higher, and at times it was almost impossible to follow amidst rocks and gorges. Benjamin began to feel increasingly fatigued, and he adopted a strategy to make the most of his energy: walking for ten minutes and then resting for one, timing these intervals precisely with his pocket-watch. Ten minutes of walking and one of rest. As the path became progressively steeper, the two women and the boy were obliged to help him, since he could not manage by himself to carry the black suitcase he refused to abandon, insisting that it was more important that the manuscript inside it should reach America than that he should.

A tremendous physical effort was required, and though the group found themselves frequently on the point of giving up, they eventually reached a ridge from which vantage point the sea appeared, illuminated by the sun. Not much further off was the town of Portbou: against all odds they had made it.

Lisa Fittko bade farewell to Benjamin, Gurland and her son, and headed back. The three of them continued towards the village and reached the police station, confident that like everyone else who had gone this way before them they would be given the permits they required to proceed by the Spanish officials. But the regulations had been altered just the day before: anyone arriving 'illegally' would be sent back to France. For Benjamin this meant being handed over to the Germans. The only concession they obtained, on account of their exhaustion and the lateness of the hour, was to spend the night in Portbou: they would be allowed to stay in the Hotel Franca. Benjamin was given room number 3. They would be expelled the next day.

For Benjamin that day never came. He killed himself by swallowing the thirty-one morphine tablets he had carried with him in case his cardiac problems recurred.

During that night perhaps he thought about the hunchback that had always seemed to have pursued him, arriving now to take him in one last fateful grasp. Had they arrived just one day before, nobody would have raised any objections to their continuing their journey to Portugal – one day later and they would have been aware that the regulations had changed. They would have been able to seek alternatives, and would certainly not have presented themselves to the Spanish police. There was only one brief interval in which they would meet the worst of all possible outcomes. And this was precisely the one they had chosen. Misfortune had triumphed, and Walter Benjamin had conceded.

For many years nothing more was known: it seemed as if all trace of his attempted flight had vanished. In the 1970s, at a time when the importance of Benjamin's work was finally being recognized, many students of his writing set off to Portbou inspired by the memoirs of Lisa Fittko, in which she had revealed to the world her part in getting him there. But they found nothing. No black suitcase, and no gravestone. Benjamin seemed to have disappeared into thin air.

Even today, amongst the welter of information available

on the internet, some of it false, like much else one finds there, there are those who repeat only this version of events. Who maintain that nothing can be known about the suitcase and its contents.

Fortunately, in addition to the internet I have friends. One of them, Bruno Arpaia, some years ago wrote a wonderful novel about Benjamin called *The Angel of History*. And he is the one who has told me about what actually happened. Because while it is true that for many years no one managed to find any trace of Benjamin in Portbou, the mystery was later clarified. The Spanish authorities had assumed that *Benjamin* was his first name (an easy enough mistake to make, since though pronounced differently it is used as one in Spain) and that his surname was *Walter*. And so they had registered him in the public archives, and then placed all documents relating to him in the court building at Figueres under the letter W.

It was then revealed that he had been buried in the Catholic cemetery and at some later date moved to a communal grave – and that all of his belongings had been recorded in a ledger, providing an apparently complete and accurate inventory. A leather suitcase (of no specified colour); a gold watch; a passport issued by the American authorities in Marseille; six passport photographs; a pair of glasses; a few magazines or periodicals; some letters; a few papers; a little money. No mention is made of typescripts or manuscripts. But those 'papers' – what did that refer to?

What Benjamin was carrying that was so precious to him? Which text, if it wasn't *The Arcades Project* he had given to Bataille or the 'Theses on the Philosophy of History' which he had entrusted to Hannah Arendt?

To this question not even Bruno Arpaia has an answer. In his novel, with fictional license, he has Benjamin hand them over to a young Spanish partisan to carry to safety. Someone who during a night in the mountains, prey to extreme cold and desperation, uses them to light a fire with which to save his life.

And fire, as I have already had occasion to remark, is a recurrent motif with regard to our lost books. As is well known, paper burns easily. But in reality, in a small town just over the border between France and Spain, in room number 3 in a small provincial hotel, it appears that no fires were lit.

There are those who doubt that the suitcase ever contained a manuscript. But what possible reason would Benjamin have had to lie to his companions in misfortune, and to drag that suitcase with him if it only contained a few personal effects? I'm convinced that there was something of real importance inside. Perhaps notes with which to continue his work on *Arcades*, perhaps a revised version of his work on Baudelaire. Or perhaps another work altogether, one that is entirely missing, that we do not even know existed.

No, Bruno Arpaia does not have the answer, but at the

end of our conversation he gives me another story, since Portbou has been the site of many more stories about lost papers.

Less than a year before Benjamin reached Portbou, amongst the half a million or so people fleeing bombardment from German and Italian planes and seeking to cross in the opposite direction to Benjamin, there was one Antonio Machado: the great and at the time, unlike Benjamin, genuinely elderly Spanish poet. Machado also had with him a suitcase, containing many poems, which he was forced to abandon there in order to reach exile in France, in Collioure, where he would die just a few days later.

Where are those poems, so compromising at the time because they were written by an enemy of the Franco regime? Where are the pages Benjamin guarded so jealously? Were they really all destroyed? All lost?

Who knows. There might still be some forgotten, yellowing papers in a wardrobe or an old chest in the attic of a house in Portbou: the poems of the old defeated poet and the notes of the prematurely aged European intellectual, conserved together, unknown even to the owner of the wardrobe or chest.

Is it too much to hope that sooner or later – by chance, scholarship or passion – someone will rediscover those pages and enable us to read them at last?

London, 1963:

I Guess You Could Say I've a Call

FEBRUARY 11, 1963: in the flat in 23 Fitzroy Road that she has rented partly because W. B. Yeats once lived there and it seemed like an auspicious precedent, Sylvia Plath wakes up very early. She always has problems sleeping when she is unwell, but has learned to turn this to her advantage, writing poems at dawn before the children are awake. The last one she has written, a few days previously, is called 'Edge' – the limit, which she has finally decided to cross. She prepares breakfast for Frieda and Nicholas (she is almost three years old; he is just one), enters their room and places two small glasses of milk and a few slices of buttered bread on a sidetable; then opens the window, even though it is cold outside, and leaves the room, sealing it after she has done so by placing a rolled up towel along the bottom edge of the door. She goes back to the kitchen, shuts herself in and seals the door in the same way she had sealed the children's bedroom. Then she opens the oven door, places a cloth on it to lay her head on, and turns on the gas.

This is how Sylvia Plath kills herself. It is the second time she has tried, ten years after her first suicide attempt.

She has recently turned thirty and is the wife of Ted Hughes, though a few months previously they separated because of his infidelity. She is not yet famous: she has published widely in magazines, and is the author of one volume of poems, *The Colossus*, and of *The Bell Jar*, a novel she published under a pseudonym. The critical reception of these books had been lukewarm.

She leaves behind a great deal of unpublished writing. As well as personal papers, diaries and letters, there is a completed volume of poems – *Ariel* – together with many other uncollected poems and the manuscript of another novel with the provisional title *Double Exposure*.

Even though they are separated, Hughes is still her husband and the legal inheritor of her literary legacy: it falls to him to determine the fate of everything she has left behind.

Whoever has read this book thus far will have gathered that I am interested in gossip: not least, perhaps, as someone once remarked, because literature itself is a higher form of gossip. But on this occasion I would like to indulge in it as little as possible. For years Hughes had to endure the accusation that he was responsible for his wife's death, as if her suicide had been an inevitable consequence of his own behaviour. Some have even pointed to the fact that the woman he left her for also committed suicide: conclusive proof of his culpability. Perhaps only when, decades later, Hughes published the poems he had written to Plath over the years in the form of birthday letters was it properly understood that things were somewhat more complicated, as of course they always are. And that behind it all, perhaps, was the fascination he had always had for women who were troubled, difficult, dark. They had been like this from the start; he wasn't the one to make them so.

But the choices made by him – so important during Plath's lifetime – have certainly contributed heavily, for good or ill, to her posthumous success, and have played a role in determining what we have been able to read and what we are no longer able to read: what we will never be able to see now.

And this is the last story of a lost book that I have decided to relate.

> I have done it again.
> One year in every ten
> I manage it…
> […]
> I am only thirty.
> And like the cat I have nine times to die.
> This is Number Three.

This is how 'Lady Lazarus' begins, one of the last poems by Sylvia Plath who did not, unfortunately, enjoy the luck afforded to cats, dying at the third 'life'. The first had been not a suicide attempt but an accident she had had, aged ten.

It frequently happens that when someone commits suicide, their death becomes the point of departure for reading their entire life. But this entails the risk of superimposing over the face of the actual person – the one who has lived, thought, written – a mask that squeezes the richness of their humanity and artistry into the form of an icon, into something two-dimensional.

That Plath had always flirted with death is a given. And this flirtation no doubt grew out of the kind of fragility that is evident in her diaries – but also from a defiance, a strength, a capacity to struggle, a controlled violence manifest in the sculpted hardness of her poems.

Much of her own experience can be recognized in *The Bell Jar*, filtered through its protagonist, in the painful trajectory from depression to attempted suicide and 'cure' by electroshock therapy. And in these pages it is possible to discern the inextricable link between suffering and guilt that was at the centre of her life and poetry, as if suffering were the responsibility of the sufferer – as well as the means of arriving at truth in writing, and being a poet. It is a narrow, high ridge to walk, one she trod for her entire existence. 'Lady Lazarus' again:

Dying

Is an art, like everything else.

I do it exceptionally well.

I do it so it feels like hell.

I do it so it feels real.

I guess you could say I've a call.

But her real vocation was writing. And this is what we need to focus on to understand what happened to her after her death.

Before doing so, however, we need to return to her relationship with Hughes. A deep relationship of love but also of literary solidarity; one in which Plath energized her husband to be a poet to his core, to make this the meaning of life, while at the same time seeking from him support in facing the agonizing creative struggle that formed the basis of her own ideas about literature. 'What I am fighting for', she wrote in a letter to her mother, 'is the strength to claim "the right to be unhappy" together with the joy of creative affirmation...', as if the two things could not be separated; as if the latter could only emerge in fact from the former. This was a kind of unhappiness Plath had carried within her for some time, since the death of her father, which left her bereaved aged ten – an avoidably early death, since he believed that he had cancer and refused medical help, when he was suffering in fact from a curable form of diabetes – an unhappiness that also originated in her difficult and conflicted relationship with her mother, in her desperate need to be loved.

What Hughes meant to her can be gauged from another letter written to her mother in 1956:

> I shall tell you now about something most miraculous and thundering and terrifying and wish you to think on it and share some of it. It is this man, this poet, this Ted Hughes. I have never known anything like it. For the first time in my life I can use all my knowing and laughing and force and writing to the hilt all the time, everything, and you should see him, hear him...

It must have been difficult for Hughes to live up to such expectations, to such a role, such love. And it is possible that he balked, ultimately, at this intensity, this altitudinous conception of both personal and artistic life.

An intensity evident from the violence of their very first encounter, when he tore the headscarf from her hair and kissed her neck – and she responded by biting his cheek. That this is not some kind of literary myth is testified by his own account of the meeting, in his poem 'St Botolph's':

> [...] I remember
> Little from the rest of that evening.
> I slid away with my girl-friend. Nothing
> Except her hissing rage in a doorway

And my stupefied interrogation

Of your blue headscarf from my pocket

And the swelling ring-moat of tooth-marks

That was to brand my face for the next month.

The me beneath it for good.

And it was to be 'this man, this Ted Hughes', who at a certain point had fled from the risks of an all-encompassing relationship, who was tasked with handling the papers Plath had left behind; papers suffused with the same vehemence from which he had sought to extricate himself.

There were diaries, including the diary of her last months in which she described her situation, her feelings, her resentments, as well as their interrupted love. (A love not ended, never at an end, as we will see decades later in the poems that Hughes wrote for her.) There were poems that included fierce attacks on her long dead father, in which he was transformed into an emblematic figure of male and even Nazi violence (he was of German origin), into an inextricable amalgam of parent and husband. There was also a substantial draft of an unfinished novel that like *The Bell Jar* was semi-autobiographical but was based on more recent experience, dealing with her unfolding life together with Hughes, and his betrayal of her with their mutual friend, Assia Wevill. Plath wrote in a letter that this novel was based on a scenario that was 'semi-autobiographical, about a woman whose husband turns out to be treacherous and a womaniser'.

What was to be done with all of these papers?

Hughes made his decisions, and they would be radical ones, destined to determine the future of Plath's work.

The first of these was to destroy the diary dealing with the last months of her life. He did this, as he later explained, because he did not want it ever to be read by their children: he was convinced that it would cause them too much suffering. (Though, tragically, this act could not prevent their son, many years later, from also taking his own life.) I have already made my own position clear with regard to decisions about destroying work intended for publication, when that work might profoundly affect people other than the author. It might be the wrong decision, but the heirs are within their rights when taking it. Plath's other diaries gradually find their way into print, along with many of her letters.

Then Hughes published *Ariel* – the book that established her reputation as a great poet – after modifying somewhat Plath's own selection of the poems to be included in it. In subsequent years he would continue to publish other poems and prose, some of it already published in magazines, a good deal of it appearing for the first time.

So what became of the unfinished novel? What became of *Double Exposure*?

We can only know from what Hughes has said about

it. According to his remark in the introduction to *Johnny Panic and the Bible of Dreams*, a collection of short stories and other miscellaneous prose by Plath, this text of 'some 130 pages' had 'disappeared somewhere around 1970'. Surely a strange enough assertion, when looked at closely. What does it mean to say that it 'disappeared'? How is it possible, given the devotion and care Hughes had dedicated to preserving and editing Plath's work, that one hundred and thirty pages of a novel could disappear into thin air with his barely even noticing?

One wonders whether this might not be a way of defending himself from accusations that he had in fact caused it to disappear: yet in the case of the diary he had no compunction in saying that he had destroyed it, and in accepting full responsibility for having done so. In this case, however, he switched between different versions of what had happened to the manuscript, having previously attributed its disappearance to Plath's mother – after her death, when she was no longer able to confirm or deny responsibility – referring to it at that time as a typescript of some sixty or seventy pages. It seems mysteriously to have doubled its length (its still-missing length) by the time of *Johnny Panic and the Bible of Dreams*.

It seems likely that Ted Hughes was not telling the truth, and faced with his reticence and contradictions it is next to impossible to know what really happened to *Double Exposure*.

'When it comes to poets, we should let their words have the last say. ' So my friend the poet Maria Grazia Calandrone tells me, when I talk to her in an attempt to clarify my ideas. Too many layers have ossified around Plath. Her life and the nature of her death have resulted in the construction of a fictional character; her own words have been overlaid by thousands of accounts by others. Even accounts by those who may never have read a line of her work, but who speak as if they had known her.

Maria Grazia reads me part of a poem written in 1997 by Frieda Hughes:

> While their mothers lay in quiet graves
> Squared out by those green cut pebbles
> And flowers in a jam jar, they dug mine up.
>
> Right down to the shells I scattered on her coffin.
>
> They turned her over like meat on coals
> To find the secrets of her withered thighs
> And shrunken breasts.
>
> They scooped out her eyes to see how she saw,
> And bit away her tongue in tiny mouthfuls
> To speak with her voice.

But each one tasted separate flesh,
Ate a different organ,
Touched other skin.

Insisted on being the one
Who knew best,
Who had the right recipe.

When she came out of the oven
They had gutted, peeled
and garnished her.

They called her theirs.
All this time I had thought
She belonged to me most.

However sensitively I have tried to proceed in this chapter, perhaps I too have joined the hordes of cannibals. Now I'm beset by doubts. If *Double Exposure* were to resurface, would it be right to publish it? To publish an unfinished novel by an author who worked with such rigour on her poems, and her other texts too, constantly revisiting and revising them, striving after the exact words, forms and rhythms? Would its publication not result in further gossip-mongering, focusing attention on the parallels between the fiction and the life, further preventing Plath from emerging in her true light, giving her over again to morbid scrutiny and the persona that has been constructed around her? Placing her yet again in the fluorescent light of that kitchen in the flat in Fitzroy Road?

Maria Grazia is smiling. If the novel were found, she says, it would be her words above all that were restored to us: the words of a poet. And then she gives me a glimmer of hope. Amongst the papers that the enigmatic Hughes deposited at the University of Georgia are some that may not be consulted until 2022, sixty years, that is, after the death of Sylvia Plath. The possibility cannot be ruled out that the lost manuscript of *Double Exposure* will be found there.

I smile too. I am prepared to wait and see.

Works Cited

Introduction

The children's books I allude to are *The Secret Garden* by Frances Hodgson Burnett and *La teleferica misteriosa* by Aldo Franco Pessina (Salani, 1937).

The quotation from Proust can be found in *Remembrance of Things Past*, trans. C.K. Scott Moncrieff and Terence Kilmartin (Chatto & Windus, 1982).

The Anne Michaels quotation is from *Fugitive Pieces* (Bloomsbury, 1997).

ROMANO BILENCHI, *The Avenue*

All of Bilenchi's books are available from Rizzoli, in editions published with the following titles: *Anna e Bruno e altri racconti; Il Conservatorio di Santa Teresa; Gli anni impossibili (La siccità, La miseria, Il gelo); Il bottone di Stalingrado; Amici.*

Vita di Pisto is published as an appendix to *Opere complete*, ed. Benedetta Centovalli (Contemporanea, 2009).

Two of Bilenchi's books are available in English: *The Conservatory of Santa Teresa*, trans. Charles Klopp and Melinda Nelson (Firenze University Press, 2005) and *The Chill*, trans. Ann Goldstein (Europa Editions, 2009).

GEORGE GORDON, LORD BYRON, *Memoirs*

The Major Works, ed. Jerome J. McGann (Oxford, 1986).
Franco Buffoni, *Il servo di Byron* (Fazi, 2012).

ERNEST HEMNGWAY, *Juvenilia*

A Moveable Feast: The Restored Edition (Scribner, 2010).

'Up in Michigan' is included in *The Collected Stories* (Everyman, 1995).

The letter to Pound is from *Selected Letters 1917–1961*, ed. Carlos Baker (Scribner, 1981).

BRUNO SCHULZ, *The Messiah*

The stories in *Cinnamon Shops* and *Sanatorium Under the Sign of the Hourglass* are included in *The Collected Works of Bruno Schulz*, trans. Jerzy Ficowski (Macmillan, 1998).

David Grossman *See Under: Love* (Farrar, Straus and Giroux, 1989).

Ugo Riccarelli, *Un uomo che forse si chiamava Schulz* (Mondadori, 2012).

Cynthia Ozick, *The Messiah of Stockholm* (Knopf, 1987).

Simha Guterman, *Il libro ritrovato* (Einaudi, 1993).

Francesco M. Cataluccio, *Vado a vedere se di là è meglio* (Sellerio, 2010).

NIKOLAI GOGOL, *Dead Souls*

Dead Souls, trans. Richard Pevear and Larissa Volokhonsky (Vintage, 1997).

The quotation from Marina Tsvetaeva, *Il poeta e il tempo*, ed. Serena Vitale

(Adelphi, 1984).

Leo Tolstoy, *Diaries Vol. I: 1847–1894*, trans. R.F. Christian (Faber, 2015).

MALCOLM LOWRY, *In Ballast to the White Sea*

Psalms and Songs, ed. Margerie Lowry (Meridian, 1975).

The Selected Letters of Malcolm Lowry, eds. Harvey Breit and Margerie Bonner Lowry (Jonathan Cape, 1967).

In Ballast to the White Sea (University of Ottawa Press, 2014).

The Voyage That Never Ends, ed. Michael Hofmann (*NYRB*, 2007).

WALTER BENJAMIN, *The Contents of the Black Suitcase*

Many of Benjamin's most celebrated essays can be found in *Illuminations,* ed. Hannah Arendt, trans. Harry Zohn (Jonathan Cape, 1970).

Bruno Arpaia, *L'Angelo della storia* (Guanda, 2001).

Lisa Fittko, *Escape Through the Pyrenees,* trans. David Koblick (Northwestern University Press, 1991).

SYLVIA PLATH, *Double Exposure*

Letters Home: Correspondence 1950–1963, ed. Aurelia Schober Plath (Faber, 1982).

Johnny Panic and the Bible of Dreams (Faber, 1977)

Complete Poems, ed. Ted Hughes (Faber, 1982)

Ted Hughes, *Birthday Letters* (Faber, 1998)

Frieda Hughes, *Wooroloo* (Bloodaxe, 1999)

INDEX OF NAMES

Adorno, Theodor, 100, 102
Akhmatova, Anna, 74
Arendt, Hannah, 100-102, 107
Arpaia, Bruno, 106-107, 126

Bataille, Georges, 99-100, 107
Baudelaire, Charles, 107
Beiderbecke, Bix, 83
Benjamin, Dora, 99
Benjamin, Walter, 7, 97,
Bilenchi, Romano, 7, 15-17, 19,
    21-22, 123-124
Bonner, Margerie, 87, 125
Buffoni, Franco, 34, 73, 124
Bulgakov, Michail Afanas'evič,
    74
Burnett, Frances Hodgson, 123
Byron, George Gordon, 25-38,
    73, 124

Calandrone, Maria Grazia, 120
Cam Hobhouse, John, 26, 32,
    33, 37

Cataluccio, Francesco, 63, 125
Centovalli, Benedetta, 18, 20,
    22, 124
Chagall, Marc, 56
Chalandritsanos, Lukas, 35
Corti, Maria, 14, 20
Tsvetaeva, Marina, 74, 79, 125

Dostoyevsky, Fyodor
    Mikhailovich, 74, 78

Edleston, John, 32, 35

Ferrara, Maria, 14
Ficowski, Jerzy, 62, 64, 124
Fittko, Hans, 102
Fittko, Lisa, 103-105, 126
Fogg, Phileas, 10

Gabrial, Jan, 86, 87, 93
Geremek, Bronisław, 63, 64
Gogol, Nikolaj, 7, 69-75, 77-79,
    89, 125

127

Gombrowicz, Witold, 56
Grieg, Nordhal, 85, 88, 89
Grossman, David, 56, 58, 125
Guiccioli Gamba, Teresa, 35
Gunther, Karl, 55
Gurland, Henny, 103, 104
Gurland, Joseph, 103
Guterman, Simha, 62, 125
Guterman, Yakov, 62

Hemingway, Ernest, 42-51
Hendrix, Jimi, 83
Horkheimer, Max, 100, 102
Hughes, Frieda, 111, 120, 126
Hughes, Nicholas, 111
Hughes, Ted, 112-121, 126

Joplin, Janis, 83

Kafka, Franz, 4, 56
Konstantinowski, Matvej, 74, 75

Landau, Felix, 55
Leigh, Augusta, 26
Lowry, Malcolm, 7, 69, 84-93, 125
Luzi, Mario, 19

Machado, Antonio, 108
Marchand, Leslie, 33
Michaels, Anne, 9, 123
Milbanke, Anne Isabella, 28
Moore, Thomas, 26, 27, 33, 36, 37, 38
Murray, John, 25, 26, 31, 33, 37

Nessi, Edoardo, 89, 93

O'Brien, Edward, 42-44

Ozick, Cynthia, 57, 63, 64, 125

Parker, Charlie, 83
Pasternak, Boris Leonidovič, 74
Pavolini, Lorenzo, 49
Peacock, Thomas Love, 27
Pessina, Aldo Franco, 123
Piersanti, Claudio, 18
Plath, Sylvia, 7, 111-122, 126
Pound, Ezra, 47
Proust, Marcel, 8, 9, 10, 100, 123
Pushkin, Alexander Sergeyevich, 70, 72

Riccarelli, Ugo, 57, 125
Richardson, Hadley, 42, 45
Rivière, Jacques, 100

Sandauer, Arthur, 59
Schulz, Bruno, 7, 56-65, 124, 125
Smirnova, Alexandra, 72
Stein, Gertrude, 43, 47
Szelinska, Josefina, 58

Tolstoy, Leo Nikolayevich, 74, 78, 125
Truchanowski, Kazimierz, 61

Vargas Llosa, Mario, 57
Veronesi, Sandro, 89, 91
Vitale, Serena, 73, 77, 125

Wevill, Assia, 117
Wilde, Oscar, 29
Witkiewicz, Stanisław Ignacy, 60

Yeats, William Butler, 111

Pushkin Press

Pushkin Press was founded in 1997, and publishes novels, essays, memoirs, children's books—everything from timeless classics to the urgent and contemporary.

Our books represent exciting, high-quality writing from around the world: we publish some of the twentieth century's most widely acclaimed, brilliant authors such as Stefan Zweig, Marcel Aymé, Teffi, Antal Szerb, Gaito Gazdanov and Yasushi Inoue, as well as compelling and award-winning contemporary writers, including Andrés Neuman, Edith Pearlman, Eka Kurniawan, Ayelet Gundar-Goshen and Chigozie Obioma.

Pushkin Press publishes the world's best stories, to be read and read again. To discover more, visit www.pushkinpress.com.

═══

BINOCULAR VISION

EDITH PEARLMAN

'A genius of the short story' Mark Lawson, *Guardian*

IN THE BEGINNING WAS THE SEA

TOMÁS GONZÁLEZ

'Smoothly intriguing narrative, with its touches of sinister,
Patricia Highsmith-like menace' *Irish Times*

BEWARE OF PITY

STEFAN ZWEIG

'Zweig's fictional masterpiece' *Guardian*

THE ENCOUNTER

PETRU POPESCU

'A book that suggests new ways of looking at the world
and our place within it' *Sunday Telegraph*

WAKE UP, SIR!

JONATHAN AMES

'The novel is extremely funny but it is also sad and
poignant, and almost incredibly clever' *Guardian*

THE WORLD OF YESTERDAY

STEFAN ZWEIG

'*The World of Yesterday* is one of the greatest memoirs of the twentieth
century, as perfect in its evocation of the world Zweig loved, as it is
in its portrayal of how that world was destroyed' David Hare

WAKING LIONS

AYELET GUNDAR-GOSHEN

'A literary thriller that is used as a vehicle to explore big
moral issues. I loved everything about it' *Daily Mail*

FOR A LITTLE WHILE

RICK BASS

'Bass is, hands down, a master of the short form, creating in a few pages
a natural world of mythic proportions' *New York Times Book Review*